Life and Survival

Survival And Life

Lessons learned

Leo Gnawa

Self-Published -By-Leo Gnawa

First Edition

ISBN: 9798524626479

.

I dedicate this book, to Chris

To Chris. Thank you for believing in yourself and being an achiever and a successful businessman, despite having dropped out of high school because of your reading disability. I get great inspiration and motivation from stories like yours and use mine to inspire and motivate others as well. When I met you, you gave me a job, which was to tell you in less than a minute, about my purpose as a writer and how my writing will contribute to change in the world. I hope you can read this book in one minute because this is the answer to your question. Thanks again. Leo

TABLE OF CONTENTS:

Introduction:

I was selling my book on 15th Street and F street Northwest Washington DC. A guy who purchased my book before stopped by with his friend. He reminded me that he had promised me that he was going to come back. I could not remember him because I talked to hundreds of people while selling my book. He told his friend about me, a homeless man selling his own books out there. His friend with a stoic posture told me that he could not read. Yet, he bought a copy of my book. He handed me twenty dollars and asked me to keep the change. I thought he was just joking. He then pulled two one hundred dollars bills and told me that he had a job for me. The job was that I had to tell him in a minute I think, what was the purpose of my book Homeless Lives Matter and how I think I could help make the world better. I was puzzled by his question, but I promised that I would work on it since he told me that I did not have to answer right away. He gave me a card with his name, email, and phone number on it, I think.

When I got to my tent later, I google-searched his name and saw a video with him telling his story. He dropped out of high school because of a learning disability. He had a problem with reading till the day I met him. I am not sure whether he was dyslexic or had another learning disability.

Days later, he stopped by again and told me that he was going home to Seattle. He got my number and left. A couple of months later, he texted me to check on me and see how I was doing. I responded and mentioned that I was working on a second book (this one), but I had left my laptops in my tent uncovered, and rain and snow had damaged it. But besides that, I was ok.

He then texted me asking me if it was ok for him to bless me with a new laptop. I was stupefied but pleasantly surprised. I accepted the offer. He asked me what exactly I wanted. I told him anything HP or Dell.

He asked me to provide him with a shipping address and he sent me a laptop. I received it the following week. I thanked him and told him that I would dedicate the book to him. I started writing this book with the laptop he offered me as a gift to write this book. Unfortunately, the computer got damaged also because I exposed it to rain. Although I ended up writing most of this book with another laptop, I really wanted to express my gratitude to him because his story was an inspiration to me. He dropped out of high school for the reasons I explained early. But he ended up creating successful businesses as a young high school dropout.

Everything I wrote in this book is all about, believing in yourself, being positive, doing what is right, treating other people as you want others to treat you, taking care of yourself and your health, and be mentally strong to survive successfully and overcome difficulties.

This book, Life and Survival, Lessons learned, is actually part two of my previous book, Homeless Lives Matter, Homeless My Story. I am contemplating writing a third book to fully tell my story. In the first book, I tried to create awareness about homelessness by telling my own experience with homelessness. In this book, I am dealing with how I survived through homelessness and finally did what I needed to do to no longer be a homeless person and to make progress in my life.

Each of the nine chapters of the book deals with one of the lessons that hard times taught me. In the last chapter, I share with you stuff that I wrote daily in the last eight months that I spent in my tent and on a friend's couch as a homeless to the day I made enough money to afford a place to live.

My purpose is to inspire and motivate you through those lessons so that you can overcome the issues that are causing you, anxiety and stress, and preventing or delaying your progress towards achieving your goals in life.

CHAPTER I

That I have to know myself

(Understand your reality, make intelligent decisions, be logical, be open-minded, seek guidance on how to deal with life better, make progress and be successful in life)

One of the lessons that tough life has taught me is to be real with myself, which means to know myself. To know myself means to know what is wrong or right with me. What causes me to react the way I do to certain situations. To know myself is to know, what my reality has been from childhood to now, as far back in time as I can remember, and how it has affected me in any way, shape or form. There are things that I will not share with anyone unless I trust someone enough and see the necessity to do so. But I have learned not to repress or deny what I know about myself..

Getting to know myself helped me address issues that were depressing, stressing, and preventing me from making progress. Today, things are better for me because I learned from the lessons that life taught me through hardship. But it was not the case not long ago. I wrote a book called Homeless Lives Matter: Homeless My story; in which I discussed my experience with homelessness. But I did not share a lot of details that I will share now, without repeating everything that I wrote in the other book. I want you to know what I went through, then I can better explain how I used the lessons learned to make progress in my life. I am doing this because I believe that you can also apply these lessons in your life and become happy with your reality.

A few months ago, I was a chronic homeless and hopeless. Now, I am no longer homeless. I sold thousands of copies of my book and made enough money to accomplish a lot in life and also inspire and motivate thousands of folks around the world. I am not there yet as far as claiming success is concerned, but I am on my way by making progress. The stage of reality I am in now as far as living in this physical realm and on this planet as a human being is concerned, is not success yet but progress towards it. Progress because I moved out of the undesirable condition I was living in, which was, not having a place of my own but living in a tent or on someone's couch and not having a reliable and sustainable source of income. Today, I am able to keep a roof over my head and have a place of my own, and am able to earn enough to take care of my basic needs. But I am not where I ideally would like to be yet, which is having enough means to be self-sufficient, self-reliant, and financially independent to say the least. The ideal reality that I need to reach in order to consider myself a success, is not just about making enough money, having a nice place, eating well, and accumulating material possessions. Success is all of these things plus. What is plus? I will get to that later. But let me get back to what I am trying to share with you in this book, which is the lessons I have learned through going through hell.

I am not here to tell you how to live your life or how to solve your problems. That will be a very arrogant thing for me to do. I am not here to play a psychiatrist or psychologist. I have no training in mental health or behavioral science. I am not an expert in anything, and I don't even have a college degree. I am just a regular guy who has gone through a hard life for a long time and finally figured a way out of misery. Now, I am fine and want to share with you the lessons that I have learned that help me overcome the barriers on my path. So, if this book can be a source of inspiration and motivation to you, then I have accomplished my purpose.

I am only here to share my experience with you and what worked for me. Maybe the path I took is not the path for you. But you still can learn from what I am sharing here. Each of us can learn from one another's experiences and stories. That, I believe.

I want you to find inspiration and motivation in what I am sharing with you because everything I am sharing here is based on my life story and the progress I made from overcoming difficulties and desperation. I went through hell for a long time. You can check my book Homeless Lives Matter and you will know what I am talking about. But here is what my reality was before I made progress.

I AM A ROTTEN FRUIT:

I was selling copies of my book, Homeless Lives Matter: Homeless My Story, on the street's sidewalk between F Street and G Street on 15th Street. A person approached me to check on my book. I don't even remember whether that person bought a copy or not. But we had a conversation and I told them that I was like a rotten fruit. But before I explained what I meant, the person interjected, "No, don't say that about yourself". "Hold on, let me explain what I mean," I told them while smiling.

My life up to now is a total failure. Look at me, a homeless man at age 54, still single, no college degree, living outside in a tent and homeless, therefore a total failure while most folks of my age lived an accomplished life, and are talking about retiring. while I am still trying to make it to where they were 20 years ago. That is why I call myself a rotten fruit.

I am being honest with you. Yet, you see me here selling copies of a book I wrote on my experience as a chronic homeless. Chronic homeless means I have been homeless for a long time. A time so long that when people ask me how long I have been homeless, I just lie and tell them 4 or 5 years. Yes, I have been homeless off and on for a long time, meaning, sometimes I could find a room for rent, or stay with friends, but always ended up back with nowhere to live. So that is what being a rotten fruit means.

I dropped out of college 30 some years ago after I ended up in a coma after a suicide attempt as a young college student in Oklahoma who was suffering from depression and anxiety because I felt overburdened by working full time and taking classes full time and failing them. I was in my early twenties. One day, I came back from work, went home, thought about the bad grades I was getting, and the classes I had to take over because I failed them, and decided that I was going to take my life because I was too depressed. I was already in bed, trying to get a few hours in before going to my classes in the morning, and later to my job at a nursing home where I was cleaning old folks' rooms. I rode to the grocery store up the street from the apartment complex where I was residing in Edmond, Oklahoma not far from Central State University, the school I was attending as a sophomore. I relocated there from another University in Michigan where I was a freshman. But this is a story for another book.

Once in that store, I purchased a bunch of sleeping pill packs. I am wondering today, why the person at the register did not wonder why this young man that I was, was purchasing all these sleeping pills. I drove back home in the Toyota corolla I had, got inside my apartment, got a glass filled with water, went to my bed, sat on it, tried to dissuade myself about doing this, but ended up opening the packs and swallowing almost all the pills from the all the packs I had bought. Maybe twenty, or thirty pills, I can't remember. Then, as I was getting dizzy and about to lose consciousness, a voice kept telling me, give yourself a chance, give yourself a chance. Then, I got up and as my vision became blurry and I was getting weak, I grabbed my car's key, headed downstairs, and drove a couple of blocks away to the house of an old lady who was a counselor at my school and who was like a mother to me. I was lucky I did not end up in an accident because I could barely ahead of me or hold my head straight. I made it to her front yard lawn and parked awkwardly in the yard in front of her house. My head was on the wheel, and I tried to press hard on the horn. Then I don't know what happened next. But I heard some firemen talking to me by calling my name. I guess they reached for my driver's license, or maybe the lady came out and told them my name. But I know I heard one of the firemen holding my hand and taking my pulse and telling me to try to open my eyes and look

4

at him while a face mask was put on my face. And then, I thought I died right there. A few days later, I woke up out of a coma in a hospital. How many days later? I don't remember. But, when I first recovered consciousness, is when I started pulling the tube that was inserted in my male genital for urination. It was painful doing that, I remember. But I had no idea that I was in a hospital or for what reasons. My memory came back days later when I opened my eyes to the sound of some voices, and dizzyingly saw the old lady from my school with a doctor next to her. Fainted back into sleep. And woke up from there sometime after that and became fully conscious since.

After fully recovering, the old lady, I don't remember her name, picked me up and took me to her house because I was still convalescent. I still was very weak and could barely remember anything. After a few days at her place and getting plenty of rest, I told her that I wanted to go back to my place. She insisted that I give it more time till I feel much better and that my presence at her place was no burden on her at all. But I was worried that my friends, also students at the same school, would drop by my place and worry about me because they had no idea what happened to me. I ended up going back to my apartment a few days later. My friends did come by and wondered where I was because they found my door opened and no one inside. I don't know what I told them.

It was the end of the school academic year, and I did not go to class or take my exam because I was still convalescent, and my memory was terrible. I enrolled in a treatment with a psychiatrist, but he came to the conclusion that I was doing great and did not need to come to treatment if I did not want to. I opted out. I did not enjoy sitting in a circle and telling my story to other patients suffering from severe depression.

I just promised myself that I would never attempt to take my life ever no matter what circumstance. I even got on my knees and made a prayer to use this second chance to use my life to serve others and make a positive contribution to humanity before death comes and gets me of its own will.

Although I was getting better and better, as far as recovering my senses was concerned, I still had a serious memory issue. I had a problem remembering my apartment number, my phone number, and any other important numbers right away. I also started having panic attacks. I remember one day, while I was at the same store where I had bought all these sleeping pill packs, I started feeling sick and felt like I was about to die. I was with my friend who was also my neighbor. I told him that I needed to go to the hospital. I was breathing hard as if I had a severe asthma attack. Actually, I was born with asthma and had it very back from my birth until I turned about 17 years and it totally disappeared. So, I never had any asthma attacks since that age. But I do have asthma-like attacks when I am exposed to cat hair or ashes. But, in that store, it was not the case of me being exposed to anything I was allergic to. The ambulance came and took me to the hospital. I was told that I had a panic attack and also told that anytime I experience the same feelings of urgency to go seek medical attention and with increased heartbeats, I should grab a brown paper bag and breath in and out of it. I was told that when having panic attacks, more carbon dioxide is exhaled, and having an imbalance in breathing oxygen in and carbon dioxide out can cause paralysis on parts of my body and cause serious physical harm. I was told that anxiety was the cause of the panic attacks I was experiencing.

Obviously, I was still very anxious about not being in school and having to redo during the following year, the entire academic year was lost at that time.

We were in the summer then and I started going back to work part-time cleaning offices at night. One weekend night, my friends and I decided to go out to a bowling alley each riding his car. I wanted to ride my own car. But as we're heading to the place, I remember that I had to pick up another guy who was a student also at my school and had worked at the nursing home where I used to work. He did not have any transportation and I had committed to picking him up on certain days when nobody else was available to do so. So, I told my friend that I will meet them later at the bowling alley because I had to pick someone up from work. I started rushing towards Oklahoma City from Edmond where I was. I came underneath a bridge and stopped at the stop sign. I was about to make a left turn when out of nowhere and all of the sudden, I got hit on my side of the car by a big car. My car dragged to the other side of the street but never turned over. My head was banging all over the car, but I never got thrown out of my seat because I had my seatbelt on. But I thought I was about to meet death again.

But I came out of the car uninjured. Unfortunately, the car was totaled. There was a huge dent on the passenger side but miraculously, I came out safe from that car.

I thought my life was nothing but bad luck over there in Oklahoma. So, I decided to come to visit some friends in Washington DC for the rest of the summer. I never left dc. That was 30 years ago. A month or two after being in DC, I started looking for a job.

I was staying with friends on Queens Chapel Road, In Mount Rainier, Maryland, minutes from the Washington DC line. I walked around the area one day and saw a Kentucky Fried Chicken restaurant and walked inside and asked whether they were hiring. The manager told me to come behind the counter to an office and file an application form after talking to me and hired me on the spot. I came in for training and had been frying chicken there for a year.

One day, I woke up and felt so depressed. I was just tired of frying chicken for at least 8 hours every day of the week except for two days off. I felt like I would never have a chance to complete my studies since I had to put so much time into working to pay my share of the rent and take care of myself. Besides, I was not able to save any money during all the time I put into working full time working in the kitchen frying chicken at such a young age. It seemed like my dreams of having multiple PhDs were vanishing.

So, I stayed on the mattress on the floor that I was sleeping on and never went to take my shower and head to work as I usually would do every early morning. I never called the job and never talked to my boss about quitting.

We did not have cell phones then. You either had to use a payphone or call from a house phone. My roommates and I did not have a phone in the apartment. And also, we had to go pick our checks up at the store. We did not have the option of your paycheck being directly deposited into your bank account.

When I had to pick up my next check a couple of weeks later, I sent one of my roommates to pick it up. When he brought it back to me at the apartment, he said to me that the store manager was very worried about me and insisted that I was always welcome to come back to work any time I felt like returning.

I kept looking in the employment section of the Washington Post advertisement pages, for a job after I started feeling broke and in need of immediate income.

I saw an ad in the advertisement section of the Washington Post about traveling around the country as salespersons selling magazine subscriptions. There was no internet then as today where folks could order their magazines online or just subscribe online.

Back then, people were getting their news from their town or city's daily newspapers at the newsstand or by delivery at their home. But for weekly or monthly magazines or periodicals, folks will purchase them at convenience or grocery stores, or simply have their subscriptions delivered through the mail. So, some smart couple that I ended up working for, for a month, decided to entice young people with the fantasy of traveling while making money by selling books and magazines. What they used to do is get to a city, put ads in local papers, ask folks that were of a certain age, I guess 20 to 25 year-olds or something like that, you enroll and travel and make money. I called them and had to meet them somewhere here in Washington DC, where they were picking us to take us to a hotel near Baltimore. Sorry, a motel shall I say.

Once the 5 or 6 of us, young men in their twenties that they picked in Washington DC, got to the motel near Baltimore, they put us in motel rooms where we had to share rooms with one or two other persons in a two-bed bedroom. In the morning, we had to participate in some meetings lasting an hour. The meeting was about telling us how to go door to door and sell magazines. After the meeting, we were given $5 and taken to an area where there was some fast food. So, we had to feed ourselves with those five dollars and then be divided into different teams in a couple of vans that would drop each of us on a particular block with a portfolio containing pictures of different publications and magazines. We had to go door to door to sell subscriptions. We were paid a percentage of the subscription we sold. I don't remember how it was. But those who did not sell anything or enough could draw five or ten dollars on credit per day, I think. I am not too sure of the precise amount. But, if a young man or lady could not make enough to cover the money they were drawing after a certain time, they would have been sent back home with nothing but a Greyhound bus ticket from wherever they were at. From Baltimore after working in the surrounding towns, we went to Columbia, South Carolina.

While working there, I knocked on the door of a middle-aged man. He did not purchase any book, but he seems mesmerized by my person. He told me that he was in very poor health and that being in my presence, he felt some great empath. He told me that I sound seek to work with terminally ill people because, according to him, I seem to have a gift of making people feel hopeful. I found his whole demeanor and discourse quite strange. He was always in tears when I left his porch to the knock on the next door, with the hope of feeling luckier there. But, up to today, I am trying to make sense of his words, and find a purpose in them. In actuality, I can say today that I feel so happy when folks who read my previous book, Homeless Lives Matter: Homeless My Story, and also followed me on social media, mainly on my Instagram page by the same name, found inspiration and motivation in my words and story.

But back to the story. Although I was getting 4 or 5 subscriptions per day, I was making barely enough for 3 meals a day and nothing to save. Most of the young men and women doing this were not making enough money to really earn enough. Obviously, the guy and his wife who were hiring us were only exploiting the young and naïve folks that were. To many of the young folks, it was just a means to travel and see different states while not worrying about paying for accommodations. But in reality, the total of subscriptions they were selling per day as a group was bringing enough profit for the couple we worked for. When we got to Orlando Florida, I started thinking about returning to Washington DC and trying to find something better to do than being used by some bad people of my own complexion. What really disgusted me was that those folks were putting 4 of us in a bedroom with two beds. Which means that we're forced to share a bed with someone else or just lay on the floor. And then they would wake us up very early in the morning for a meeting at around 8 am and then get us on the road an hour later and then pick us up around 4 pm and bring us back to the motel by 5 or 6 pm. We then had to report whatever sales we made and get whatever payment we were owed. So, we just had time to go get some to eat, and then it was night and time to sleep to get enough rest and strength for the following. I told them I had to go. We were still on the east coast, and I didn't want to go further from the East Coast. They had somebody take me to the greyhound station in Orlando, Florida, and put me on the bus with nothing but whatever few dollars I had on me. I returned to DC with nowhere to go. I returned to the apartment that I was sharing with my roommates, but they had moved out. But luckily, I walked by a building, and some young brothers who were friends with some of my roommates recognized me and told me that my roommates had moved out. It was ok for me to come and stay with them. They were 4 brothers sharing the apartment. One of them was also called Leo and we became very close friends in no time. Actually, I felt like all of them were my brothers. Leo was about my age and the three others were younger.

I was recommended to someone who owned a tire shop in Gaithersburg, Virginia. He hired me and even offered me to stay in the store since he had a little room with the bed upstairs and a bathroom downstairs with a shower. So, I stayed and worked there. Then one of the workers there who was my buddy asked me if I was willing to move in with him in a two-bedroom apartment he was willing to rent. I accepted. We moved together on 13th and Euclid Street in Northwest Washington DC. The tire shop owner let my friend drive one of his old vehicles so that we could get to the job by 6 am and open the shop by 8 am. It was about an hour's drive to the shop.

The man was paying me $5 per hour. It was a hard job. But I did it for a good year. But again, one morning I was very depressed about working so hard for that little money for an entire year. I was earning just enough to pay my share of the rent and get some food. I could not save anything. That was depressing to me to work hard and never have enough money for anything else than rent and food. So, one morning, I woke up and told my friend that I quit and never went back to work. This is what depression does to you.

I had gotten some money from my mother in the meantime and survived on it until my friend moved out of state to attend college in Virginia. So, I was in the apartment by myself with no job and unable to pay rent. I ended up being evicted. That was about 20 some years ago when I first found myself with nowhere to live. But I didn't stay on the street for too long. I had met the mother of my daughter who was a few years younger than me. She and I managed to stay here and there at somebody's place until we found a room that somebody rented to us. Then later we were able to stay at a few places for free.

We ended up going our separate ways. I ended up going from one homeless shelter to another, from Blair Shelter in Northeast to Randall Shelter in Southwest, to Second and D Shelter in Downtown Washington DC to another shelter in Ivy City. To New York Avenue Shelter.

Then, as I was working on day jobs on construction sites, I was able to find a room to rent on the corner of New York Avenue, Northwest Washington DC. The owner was the perfect definition of a slumlord. The place was rat-infested. When I used to come home, as soon as I opened the door, a rat

11

would just race in front of me to the steps till upstairs. I am not talking about mice. I am talking about big fat rats. There were five rooms upstairs with one bathroom and one fridge for all of us to share. One day, I had bought some ice cream and put it in the freezer, and went to my room to rest after I came from work as a day laborer. When I decided to eat some of it, I went and opened the freezer and found an empty ice cream box in the freezer. There was no need to go ask the other guys renting rooms there, who ate my ice cream. It would be a waste of time because no one will come forward and admit to eating it. Also, many of the guys there were having visitors from the street coming up there. So, it could be anybody who does not live there but is visiting from the street who simply ate the ice scream with others.

But that was not the real problem for me. One day, I came home and was told that there had been an electric fire in the building and the firemen had busted my door to get to the roof of the building. The doors did not really have locks. We were using padlocks to lock our doors. The landlord did not have the decency to even temporarily cover the hole in my roof. I had to go back outside and find some cardboard and manage to put them on top of the hole in my roof and sit some bricks on the edges to secure them from being blown out by high winds. The electricity was cut off in the building for almost a month. The landlord never cared to repair and fix it. We remained in the dark all that time, but he had the nerves to wants to collect rent every Friday since we were paying him weekly. We had no choice but to pay him, otherwise he would put an extra lock on the door to prevent us from getting inside our rooms.

I personally got tired of paying him while I was getting drenched during heavy rains leaking through the roof.

I just took whatever I cared for out of the room and went to join my homeless friends in the alley of the back of buildings on New York Avenue and 13th street, in Northwest Washington DC. I found a spot in a garage there and was sleeping there every night.

But back to where I started. When I said to that person in front of me that I was a rotten fruit, I meant that a long period of my life was spent in suffering and going through hard times with no accomplishment whatsoever over more than 30 years. But I wanted her to understand that I was using that rotten fruit analogy to express to him that I was using my experience with suffering as a means to turn that bad experience into a success story.

But, me being out there on the street selling my book, was to me, an opportunity I had created for myself to find a way out of the miserable life I had endured all these years.

The rest of the story is that I took the rotten fruit, planted it into fertile ground, watered it, and turned it into a tree.

Today, my life is no longer a rotten fruit. I am now a rotten fruit that grew into a tree about to bear fruits. As I said earlier, you have to know yourself. All that time that I was going through a hard time, I couldn't clearly focus on a solution because I was stressed out and depressed about my reality. It took me to take the time to look at my life and accept the reality I was dealt with.

I had to tell myself, Leo, instead of being here stressing yourself about what you have not accomplished and everything you went through, why don't you figure a solution out by using what is potent in you as talent or natural gifts? This is where knowledge of self comes to play.

If you are in a tough situation and feel like there is no way out, whether it is poverty, ailment, relationship, or life in general, I can assure you that you are mistaken. Look deep within yourself. You have inside you what you need to deal with the situation and make things better. Fear, lack of knowledge of self, lack of self-confidence, and stress are what hinder us from looking inwards for what it takes to solve problems. When I understood that, it was easy to start looking within myself for the tools to deal with my issues and make progress.

One day, in 2005, while I was still homeless, I was thinking of starting a homeless newspaper, but I learned from another homeless person whom I was sharing the idea with, that there was a homeless newspaper in Washington DC called Street Sense. I went to the church where the newspaper was located. A young white male welcomed me upstairs. He was the founder of the newspaper. I expressed my interest in writing for the paper and also selling it on the streets. He invited me to use one of the few computers in the office to write. I sat on one of them and started writing. I also started selling the paper the next day. I know it was quite embarrassing for me to be on a street corner selling a homeless newspaper. By doing so, I was exposing myself as a homeless person. But I put my price on the side and looked at the bigger picture. I had come to the realization that our pride can be in the way of our progress. To me, the most important thing was to be able to write in the paper and come in contact with customers of the paper who will read my articles. I figured that if I was able to write great articles, it would not only help my sales but also expose me to an audience that I can create for myself. So, I cast my pride aside and focused on the greater plan. A few days later, I started vending the paper on the street after being trained by another vendor for a day or half a day, not so sure. I started at the Dupont Circle Metro Station. And from there, I walked inside the Dupont Circle Park and approached folks sitting either on the circular benches, or on the lawn, or around the statue in the center of the park. From there, I headed to the Wholefood, on P street by 14th street Northwest. I established that as my daily routine. It did not take long before I established a faithful clientele, mainly made of my regular readers. Obviously, many of those who purchased my copies liked my articles in the column section.

I want to share with you two of the articles I wrote in 2005 in Street Sense. Both articles were liked by many of my customers.

Street Sense Newspaper, May 15, 2005

Be Like a Wizard! Make it Happen!

by LEO GNAWA

Well, like everybody in the metropolitan area of Washington, D.C., I was happy about the success of the Washington Wizards for making it to the play-offs. Yet, the attitude of some of its players has me wondering whether success necessarily leads to happiness.

When I look at my 39-year-life experience, it is pretty much a failure, since it has ended in the opposite direction of where I ever idealized my life to turn out to be, and as a result, I can only feel unhappiness. Because of that, in my opinion, happiness can only come about when success knocks on my door.

Yes, I said "success" of the Wizards, although the D.C. basketball team has not been able to defeat the Miami Heat in the second round. At least they made it to the play-offs and to round two. That achievement is a success. It is true that not everybody who is successful is happy. To me, that is because success can only bring happiness when we look at success as gradual instead of absolute. The attitude of Kwame Brown, who went straight from high school into the NBA, is a clean illustration of what I mean. Sometimes, people take the little things they possess for granted. Think of those who have nothing, and then you may appreciate the little things you are fortunate enough to have in your possession.

Well, thanks to ESPN Zone, I missed only a few of the Wizards play-off games. It only cost me about $3 for a glass of Pepsi to stay inside. Although I once just slipped inside the venue, took the elevator down to the first lower-level floor and mingled in with the crowd watching the game on the big screens. Many homeless people feel a little embarrassed to go inside such an establishment. They fear some homeless-sniffing employee or security office might walk up to them and say, "No loitering. Only customers allowed. You got to get out. Now!" But I did not have to worry about such embarrassment because I made sure I appeared presentable and always carried enough money to afford the cheapest beverage available. By doing so I didn't allow anyone to deny me the right to be there as a customer – whether I am homeless or not.

People are judged by how they look and how they conduct themselves. Although appearance is external and can give others the wrong impression of us, attitude is internal and shows what we are within. Attitude shows our true self. Nonetheless, the right appearance and attitude will surely lead anyone down the path of success. Attitude is really what I want to focus on in this reflection about success. The attitude of Kwame Brown shocked me. I would expect the Wizards' 23-year-old power forward to just be happy that he and his teammates made it to the play-offs. But instead, he skipped out to protest against the Chicago Bulls, after two game losses in Chicago. By faking a stomach virus and not showing up for a practice, a shoot-round, and the second home game, Kwame Brown earned himself a suspension for the rest of the play-offs.

What a smart way to jeopardize a career with a promising future, not only with his current team but also with any prospective team that might have entertained any interest in him. This is what I meant earlier when I said success only brings happiness when we see success as gradual instead of absolute. I did not read this somewhere. It is what I believe, and Kwame Brown's attitude illustrates that point very well. Here is a young man who is not appreciating his blessings because things are not as perfect as he desires. Now what does it matter whether your coach gave you five or 40 minutes during a game? Coaches coach, and players play. So, this young man should have respected his coach and appreciated any opportunity he had on the court. I am quite sure that Peter Ramos, who plays for the Wizards and was not added to the teams' playoff roster, was still happy to belong to a team that was successful enough to advance to the play-offs. At least he understands that his success is gradual. He knows that he has made it to one step and is willing to take it from there until next season, when he develops enough to earn more play time.

Those who are blessed with some fortune, financial security, good health and a full and stable life, should think of those who have nothing and are totally deprived, like the homeless, the poor and those suffering. Whining and complaining will not make things better but worse. I wish somebody would offer me $30 million to sit on a basketball team bench. Kwame

Brown don't mess your luck up. With your attitude, you may not find a team willing to offer you the $30 million that the Wizards did, which you turned down as a free agent. Some of us are homeless and have nothing; you are young and have everything. Be like a wizard. Make it happen. You are blessed. Be happy.

Leo has been a Street Sense vendor for four months. If you would like to send him any comments, please e-mail him at leognawa@hotmail.com.

This article was very much liked. I received a lot of emails from readers, and I responded with the following article as a response to a Russian tourist who bought the paper from a vendor and wrote me her reaction. Unfortunately, I cannot find that email in my email archives. Here is the article I wrote as a reflection on her email.

Street Sense July 15, 2005, by Leo Gnawa:

Who am I? I am Not Happy by LEO GNAWA

I want to carry on with the theme of happiness. Many readers responded positively to my column in the May 15 issue, dealing with happiness and success. One e-mail message I received was from a 20-year-old Russian tourist, who had just set foot on American soil when I first met her. Her correspondence puzzled me. She wrote, "You're much happier than many people who have everything except themselves. happiness is just a state of mind regardless of your possessions."

State of mind? I think she's right. If someone has more than enough for their daily sustenance, to maintain a stable life and to meet all their material needs, and he or she still cannot find happiness, something's wrong. I will be honest: If I had the wealth, the talent and the fame of Michael Jackson, I would be happy, and I don't care what anyone says. I am just being real.

Someone said that money is the root of all evil, but I beg to differ. I think money is all right, there is nothing wrong with money. The roots of all evil are in man's motives based on greed, selfishness and insensitivity towards others. Money is a tool just like a knife but in the mind of whoever uses the knife – same as money.

As I have stated in my previous column, my present condition is that of unhappiness because of my failure to achieve my ideals. Consequently, it is my belief that my quest for happiness can become fruitful only when I achieve success in turning dreams into reality. And all I can dream of now is material and financial stability. So, I wonder how folks like Michael Jackson do, with all their wealth and success, end up unhappy that they're engaging in weird behavior.

I have no clue what the answer is. But, when I read my young Russian friend's e-mail again, I can see an answer. She said, "You are happier than most people who have everything except themselves."

She's got a point. The truth of the matter is that I am much happier than Michael Jackson because now I would not want to be in his current predicament – despite his recent "not guilty ruling." But being accused of child molestation and having the reputation of a pedophile wouldn't make anyone happy except a psychopath. No wonder Michael flew to Bahrain, in the Arabian Peninsula with his three children right after the verdict of the child molestation trial, in what appears to be a self-imposed exile out of the United States.

What transpires from the Michael Jackson situation is that the identity crisis, which he obviously suffers from as his metamorphosis from the Negro race to the Caucasian race shows, has not allowed him to fully enjoy his good luck. By good luck, I mean talent, fame and wealth.

I am not a psychiatrist, and I will not attempt to explain Michael Jackson's mind. I understand that he has allegedly been subjected to some abuse as a child. So, this may be the reason of his problem with identity. Some say he is still a child trapped in the body of an adult, he believes he is Peter Pan (a fictional little boy character who refuses to grow up and enjoys performing magic).

However, it is obvious that Michael Jackson's identity crisis has impeded the happiness that should have been naturally resulted from his success in the universal world of music, entertainment and business. The lesson I see in this situation is that at some point we have to accept who we are and the way we are. It is better to be happy with what we have than to pursue an unattainable dream and, in the process, cause greater damage to our mental stability and our self-esteem. We can cause ourselves a lot of misery by just trying to be what we are not.

There is a lot of wisdom in what my Russian friend wrote me. I may not have anything as far as material things. But, I have me, myself, and I. As long as I keep consciousness of my integrity, then I can improve my condition sometimes in the future. Sometimes we are so focused on what we perceive as the negative part of us that we fail to appreciate the good side of us. Until we learn how to love ourselves sand accept ourselves, we cannot be happy – even if we have everything. The dissatisfaction with self will always prevail over the gratification with wealth, as is the case with Michael Jackson. When we know ourselves, we know that no matter how bad we see things within or around us, there is also something good within and around us, too.

I am not happy to be poor and homeless, and as long as that is what I identify with, I will not be happy. But despite homelessness, I still have my personality and I am quite sure there is something good in it. I should be happy I have me because there is something good in me and in all of us.

Leo has been a Street Sense vendor for four months. If you would like to send him any comments, please e-mail him at leognawa@hotmail.com.

Both articles, and mainly the last one, bring me to the lesson, here which is to know yourself. While I was writing these articles, I did not realize that somebody would see a good writer in me. I was just focused on expressing my emotion and not looking at writing as part of me that is a talent.

When I was selling my copies of street sense, in front of the Metro Station at Dupont Circle and at the Wholefood store on 14th street, in Northwest Washington DC, I had few regular customers who used to tell me that I was a great writer. Also, from time to time, I would go to the park in Dupont Circle and walk around and try to sell my copies of Street Sense to the folks resting in the park. I was sat by a Catholic priest who had read my article in a previous edition who looked me in the eyes and told me, you are a very good writer. I looked at him and said, "Not really". Then he admonished me for not believing in myself being a good writer.

Sometimes, we prolong our predicament because we fail to realize that we have within us, the talents and gift or ability to solve our problems.

The real problem is that we don't know ourselves. To know ourselves is to know what is unique about us, what we are naturally gifted or skilled at.

If you want to solve a lot of the issues that are affecting you, you have to know yourself, know what is unique about you, what you are naturally gifted with, what you are skilled at, what you are capable of doing in a way that most people can't.

To know yourself is also to know your weaknesses, deficiencies, and inabilities. If you don't, other people who do, will use you and take advantage of you.

Your weaknesses can be caused by your lack of knowledge of the things you need to know about your own reality. Whoever knows more than you, has an advantage over you. I will give you a simple example. There are nations and communities around the world, who are sitting on gold, diamond, and all kinds of valuable sought-after minerals, and also fertile land, but they are not valuing their natural wealth. But there are other nations and people and communities who traveled far away from across the oceans to go and conquer these people and nations to take over and control their natural resources. But the people whose lands are the richest on earth, are the poorer nations on the planet because they don't know their worth and the worth of the natural wealth they are sitting on.

The same goes with you as a person, who may have a talent, or natural gift, or even a skill or professional training, or education, but are not using your potential to earn as much as you deserve but are working for less money. You are working hard for somebody else who is ripping the benefit or your hard labor and paying you less. Then, you are working for low wages that are not equaling a living wage despite your skills, or knowledge

I will repeat again, whoever you are, there is something that you are gifted with and can do better than anybody else. And it can be anything. Some people are good at sports, others have an oratory gift and can express themselves better than others, others are just good at fixing things, and I can go on and on. But my point is, if you don't know what you are gifted or skilled at, find it out and make use of it to make your life better. Don't sit on a gold mine within you and commiserate about your undesirable condition.

For example, I like to ride bicycles, but no matter how intelligent I think I am, I don't know how to fix bicycles. So, when I have a problem with my bicycle, I have to take it to someone else to fix it for me. I might not think that the person I ask to fix my bicycle is as intelligent as me, but he has the knowledge of fixing a bicycle, and I don't. That person can be a homeless man sleeping outside, who will go panhandling to earn a few bucks to take care of his needs, while he has this skill of fixing bikes, or singing, or doing a lot of things that can be very lucrative. I will elaborate deeper in the following chapters of the book.

Let me be honest with you. One day, I was sitting in my tent and feeling depressed about being homeless and hopeless. As I was being consumed by despair, I told myself, "I am a very intelligent man, how come I can't figure a way out of this predicament that I have been in for too long?

That was the day I came to realize that the solution to the predicament I was in, was within me. For so long, I had to look outside of me, towards society or even God, to get me out of this miserable reality that I seem unable to get out of.

I came to the conclusion years later that the solution to my problems resides within me and not outside of me. To know myself allows me to have ideals and purpose and set up goals to achieve them.

CHAPTER 2

THAT I HAVE TO HAVE A PURPOSE AND GOALS

(Have goals and a purpose and seek to accomplish them while you are still alive and still have time)

Survival and hard life taught me that I have to have a purpose in life, otherwise, the life I live is just survival and struggle with no real happiness but only stress.

Many times when I walked by a cemetery, mostly at night, I stepped closer to the fence and spent few minutes there to meditate and reflect about the fact that I am here in this human reality for a brief time, and that I will also die sooner or later. To be honest, I am not afraid of death although I do not wish to die. What I am more afraid of. is to die without having accomplished anything in my life. As I am aging (I am 55-year-old now), I realize that time is going so fast and I don't have much time left. There are things in life that if you do not do now, it will be too late later. If you are a young person, finish your education instead of keep dropping out of school and keep hoping that you have enough time to go back and finish your education later. One of the things that I regret the most in my life is that I never finished my education. I dropped out of my second year of college. I would have loved to have a couple of PhD's by now. But it is ok. I am still happy, my first book reached thousands of people and hopefully thousands more find inspiration and motivation in this current book. If I die today, my books will survive me. Thousands of years from now, my books will still be here and keep me alive in the memory of generations to come.

I am therefore satisfied somehow that I still was able to accomplish something that will survive me, although I did it later than sooner because of all the difficulties I went through. I see a lot of young people who are homeless. Some of them look teenagers. And I wonder, why aren't they in school? If you are a young man or lady who are not working and not in school, please do something with your life. Don't just be content about living day to day with no purpose. You are wasting precious time, by doing nothing with your life but instead just hanging all day, every day around with friends, smoking weed all day, and listening to music that is promoting disrespect of women who could be your mothers, sisters and daughters by referring to them as female dogs; and violence against other people that looks like you. You have to have a purpose and some goals that you need to accomplish to give some meaning to your life.

And this goes for everybody. Let us value time because there is so much we can accomplish for ourselves if we plan things with discipline and understanding that time is shorter than we realize. What we call time is nothing but the movement of the earth around the sun. Once the earth goes around the sun one time, which happen every 365 days, we call it a year. Whether we do what we have to do or not, the earth is not going to stop moving around the sun to wait for us. Your body will tell you when your time gets shorter. When you age, you will not be as strong as you use to. You will not move as fast as you use to. You will get sicker and sicker as the earth continues to do more circling around the sun. There are things you can do today that you cannot do later. While you still have time, try to accomplish something with your life instead of wasting it if that is the case as far as you are concerned.

If you want to live a successful and fulfilling life, you need to have a purpose and do what you need to do to achieve your purpose. Simple as that. I told myself that while I was homeless living in a tent or sleeping on somebody's couch for a decade. And I am telling you that if you are not happy with your life, because you are still struggling to survive and have not accomplished your purpose if you have any to start with.

There is no question that to live a life as normal as possible, you need to learn how to survive and take care of your basic needs. If you are having difficulties surviving in this world that is becoming more and more complicated, then your life is going to be very hard, miserable, and depressing. I will address survival in another chapter.

Animals can survive by using their natural instinct to seek food, protect and defend themselves from danger. But most animals are not just surviving. They are playing a role in the ecosystem by interacting with the environment to make life sustainable on this planet.

Life is possible on earth because every single being, from the invisible microbes to the immense planets and stars far above us, is playing an essential role in life on earth. If the tiny bees decided to survive with no purpose as some of us human beings do, then 180,000 plant species will not be fertilized because pollen will not move from one flower to another on their own.

We cannot just reduce our existence to feeding, clothing, sheltering and entertaining ourselves, and gratifying our sexual needs. Unlike other species in the animal kingdom, you and I, humans are endowed with greater potential, greater intelligence, and a creative spirit that supersede our reliance on instinct alone for survival and therefore give us the responsibility and ability to play a greater role towards nature and towards humanity.

You and I may not end up as the heroes and venerated individuals whose names are given to buildings, schools, bridges, institutions, towns, cities, countries, rivers, and lakes because of their exceptional contribution to society and life in general. But we can find our purpose on this earth and live a productive and fulfilling life, and contribute to the betterment of humanity at least, and leave a good memory of us after we are dead and gone. Otherwise, our existence will be less meaningful than that of animals trying to survive in the wilderness.

Whoever created you and I gave us a powerful brain that no other existing beings possess. Let us use it to think hard about the meaning of your existence on this earth and what our purpose must be. Don't just live life day to day and just worry about what you going to eat the next hour, where you are going to sleep tonight, what music you are going to listen or dance to all day, and who you are going to have sex with. There is more to your existence on earth than your day-to-day survival. You are here for a purpose, just like the bees, the ants, and every other creature. Find your purpose and your survival will be meaningful.

It was a time when I felt like my life was doomed. I felt like I was living from one day to the next day and was surviving and not living to achieve any purpose. And I was not happy living like that because it became a way of life. If that is your experience with life, tell yourself as I did, "I cannot live to just survive. I must find my purpose on earth and be happy while contributing to make the world a better place and leave a positive impact long after I am gone."

Today, I am a self-published author who has sold thousands of copies of my first book, Homeless Lives Matter, Homeless My Story to a worldwide audience and who also has created awareness about the issue of Homelessness as an activist who was also homeless and is no longer since February 2021. Although I feel like this is just the beginning of a journey towards a greater purpose, I am very happy with the progress I have made in life so far.

I feel so good when people who read my book let me know how it enlightened them and changed their whole perspective about homelessness.

I heard the man say something about the homeless guy who sells his book around here. He was a middle-aged white professional-looking well-dressed man. He was leaving the restaurant at Old Ebbitt Grill and stopped in front of a guy shining shoes in the front outside. "I bought a book from a homeless writer outside here the last time I was here. Have you seen him today? I heard him, although I was about 30 feet away. I got up immediately and walked straight to him through the sizable crowd that had folks hanging out for a cigarette break and people going in and out of Old Ebbitt Grill. He had his back turned towards me. The shoeshine guy pointed at me, "You talking about him?" "I am so happy to see you. Your book changed my life. I used to not care about the homeless until I read your book. It changed me. Now, I am committed to helping the homeless" said the man to me. That made me so happy to hear that from a reader of my book "Homeless Lives Matter: Homeless My Story."

Although making enough money to get a place to live was my immediate goal, which I was still working on, to be hearing from an affluent reader of mine, that my work transformed him from a person who had apathy for the homeless to someone who has now committed to helping them, made me feel so proud and so happy.

To me, happiness is the ultimate goal. If you struggle every day to survive but you are not happy with your life, you will feel like you are not accomplishing what you idealize as success.

We all long to be happy, otherwise, even a successful life is meaningless if you still feel unhappy despite your accomplishments.

But how can you even be happy if your life is a daily struggle, and if you can barely feed yourself and meet your basic needs? I couldn't.

I had to do something that I care about, and which gives me not just inner gratification but also allows me to become self-sufficient and socially stable.

The day I decided that I needed to have a clear purpose and strive to achieve it, is when I committed to not be content with being without and with relying on charity to survive. The state of mind of not having a clear purpose in life but just worrying about food, clothes, and shelter daily, got me stuck in the predicament I was in and clouded my ability to see a better situation ahead for myself. I ended up remaining in chronic homelessness for a long time and learned how to adjust to it. It became a normal way of life for me. If you are dealing with a bad situation that has lasted so long that you have become adjusted to it, you have to convince yourself that you can overcome your dilemma and live a better life and be happy in this world. But you have to define a clear purpose for your life and define clear goals to achieve to make progress from the bad place you are to a better place you need to be.

Thinking like that motivated me to come up with a serious plan to remove myself from homelessness and achieve something with my life that will make me Self-sufficient and prosperous. Like I said, I was homeless. But since a few months ago, February 2021 to be exact, I am no longer homeless. I decided that I would give my life a purpose and come up with a plan to make it happen.

So, the question to me was, what shall I do to remove myself permanently. from chronic homelessness and be in a better situation to achieve my purpose in life. What would that purpose in life be?

In 2009, when I was selling my copies of Street Sense, the Washington DC homeless newspaper in front of the Metro Station at Dupont Circle and the Wholefoods store on 14th street, in Northwest Washington DC, I had few regular customers who used to tell me that I was a great writer. Also, from time to time, I would go to the park in Dupont Circle and walk around and try to sell my copies of Street Sense to the folks resting in the park. I sat by a Catholic priest who had read my article in a previous edition. He looked me in the eyes and told me, you are a very good writer. I looked at him and said, "Not really". Then he admonished me for not believing in myself being a good writer.

So, when I sat in my tent that day in 2016 and told myself that I had enough grey matter in my brain to figure a way out of my misery, that is when I

28

proposed myself to achieve something greater than worrying about my life and getting nowhere but getting stressed out and depressed.

Most of the time, we prolong our predicament because we fail to realize that we have within us, the talents and gift or ability to solve our problems.

I decided to use my love for writing as a tool to achieve my purpose. To me, a purpose is an ultimate ideal that we want to reach in life to feel fulfilled and become successful. The purpose is like the final destination of a traveler on a long journey. My purpose is to contribute to the upliftment of my fellow human beings, and the betterment of humanity, through activism, writing, and other actions. So, I decided to put in the work to become a successful writer and activist and reach out to millions of folks around the world.

But, even when we have an ideal purpose, we still need to have some goals and progress towards the ultimate goal which is our purpose. As I said, the purpose is the final destination of a traveler, but a goal is the next stop or next destination on the path of a traveler towards the final destination.

So, my first goal was to write a book that will accomplish two other goals. The first one was to use that book to be an active voice of awareness on the issue of homelessness based on my own experience since I was homeless still. The second purpose was to sell enough copies of that book to come up with enough money to get out of homelessness, have the means to support myself, and become stable, independent, and self-sufficient.

They were folks who used to see me on the street selling my book and thought I was not going to accomplish much doing that. One evening, I was selling my book in front of Old Ebbitt Grill. There were a lot of people outside, but I was out there for a couple of hours and not making any sales. When a man walked straight to me and stopped right in front of my books, I was relieved, thinking that he was coming to purchase a copy. "Can I talk to you?" he said. I was not interested in having a conversation. I wanted folks to stop and get a copy of my book. "Yes". I responded. Then he started telling me that there was a solution to my predicament. "What was that? "I asked him. ". He told me that there was a kingdom in heaven where there would no longer be suffering, poverty, and homelessness. I told him that I appreciated him sharing his faith with me, but I was more concerned about making sure I make enough money to take care of my daily needs and also be successful and happy here on earth. Many times, folks stopped in front of me, and instead of buying my book as I expected, they asked me where I was going to spend eternity, or whether I was saved, or there is a better hope for me by accepting Jesus and he will have a mansion for me in heaven and offer me a better life after I die. I told most of them that I appreciated what they were sharing with me, but my life was already hell on this earth and my concern was to be happy here and I was not worrying about what happens to me after death.

I was more inclined to converse with a person purchasing my book, and then taking a few minutes of my time to share his faith with me and ask me to pray with them. But when a person walked to me and did not purchase my book, but tried to sell me religion, I was not interested in hearing them. I was a homeless entrepreneur trying to make money selling my books to feed myself and get a place to live. I was not trying to hear folks who had a roof over their head telling me to wait till after I die to worry about having a roof over my head. To me that was not the proper way to try to convert me.

But back to the man who came to talk to me about the Kingdom of Heaven. He was a Jehovah Witness and he and a group of his congregation were passing Jehovah Witness literature in front of the Treasury department to tourists and folks walking to or from the front of the White House. He had come to use the bathroom inside of Old Ebbitt's and saw me on his way out and decided to preach to me although he knew I was selling my book. If he didn't know, I told him, hoping he would keep moving so I can resume my bookselling. When I told him that I was trying to solve my problem (homelessness) by selling my book, he told me that I could not make it by selling my book on the street and told me why don't you go get a job at Starbucks or somewhere like that? "Here we go again," I told myself. He was not the first one to come at me like that. Another day, I was also having a slow day. A lot of people were walking by, but very few stopped to purchase my book until a lady who was going to the restaurant told me that she was going to come back and check my book. She did come back and told me to tell her about my book and then she would decide whether to get a copy or not after. While I was talking to her, I saw a couple of old folks coming from the restaurant. The man had a twenty-dollar bill in his hand and said "I want you to make a promise to me! Promise me that you will stop wasting your time and you will go get a real job". I was disturbed and did not know what to say. The lady next to me reacted with a dejected look on her face. I babbled something like" Oh you're going to tell me writing a book and selling it is some waste of my time? Sorry sir, I don't want your money." He just put his money in his pocket and left with his wife. The lady next to me shook her head and just pulled a $20 out of her purse and handed it to me for a copy of my book. That guy unwittingly got me a sale.

Back to the Jehovah witness guy. I told him "So you want me to go work at Starbucks for $10 an hour while I sell on average 2 books within an hour, while I can sell at least 2 books within an hour on average"? The issue here is that people who are making above minimum wage and can take care of basic needs and save some of their income, fail to realize that a lot of poor people including homeless people do have a job and go work for 40 hours plus a week and are barely making it, if at all. The minimum wage in this area as in many over parts of the United States is lower than a living wage. The living wage is the minimum a person must earn to be able to take care of their basic needs according to the cost of living in their area.

Many people are poor and homeless, not because they don't have a job but because they don't earn enough to afford rent and other necessities.

"For how much do you sell a copy of your book"? the Jehovah's Witness man asked me. "$10 per copy". Oh, so you make $20 an hour selling your book? Yes, sir, I told him. Sometimes, more, sometimes less, but 2 copies, is what I sell per hour on average. And I am trying to save enough to get a place although it is not easy.

At that point, he realized the seriousness of me being out there selling my book. He had no more words. He told me that he would come and talk to me another time and that he was going to rejoin his group passing out brochures in front of the treasury department and next to the White House.

In another chapter, I will discuss what it took me to write a book and sell it and become successful.

But now, I want to focus on having a purpose and achieving it through successfully setting up goals.

You cannot and should not just live life without any purpose and just survive with no ambition or desire for a better life. You have to have a dream of an ideal reality and try to materialize it.

I know you have goals that you want to be accomplished; getting a good job and/or a promotion, finding a lover and getting married, or having children, in case you don't have those yet. Maybe earning enough money, being able to travel somewhere, just getting into a better situation in life.

But what is your ideal for real success? As I said before, you have to have a purpose in life. The goals that I listed above are not your ultimate purpose. Your ultimate purpose in life, which your goals can help you achieve, should be based on your ideal of what is the perfect situation you want to achieve.

In my case, my ideal was to be a successful writer and activist. Therefore, my goals were to earn enough money through selling my book to get a place to live and be in a better situation to move forward.

Whatever goals or purpose you have in life, plant the seeds in fertile soil and water them. You will see your plans materialize slowly but surely.

When I was telling the lady that I was a rotten fruit, at that time, I had planted the seed of the rotten fruit in the ground. What does that mean? That meant that I had a dream about what I was trying to do to improve my condition and no longer live on the street and be indigent. Today, I am no longer homeless because I was able to sell enough books to get myself out of homelessness.

First, everything starts in the mind with a dream of something we desire to accomplish to feel fulfilled. By the dream, I am not talking about what you are seeing and experiencing as reality in your subconscious mind while your body is totally in a state of deep sleep. Here I am using dream figuratively to mean a clear idea about what you want to achieve in life or what you desire to happen in the future that will fulfill your expectations.

Because you idealize something does not mean that it will just happen. To idealize something means that you entertain in your mind the desire to become what you want to be, or have what you want to have, or get to where you want to get and when you want that to happen.

A dream is something that makes you feel good in your mind and gives you hopes and expectations. But a dream does not just become reality just because we expect it to.

A dream can either be a vision, an illusion, or a nightmare. A vision is a future event or occurrence that we can dream of long before the time it happens. Let me rephrase it. A vision is a dream that we can turn into reality because we can be realistic, commonsensical, and pragmatic in the planning and execution of our dream. By dream, I mean what we think about and desire to happen in reality. What you desire in life, cannot just come into existence magically simply because you wish so. It is great to dream about something desirable, but all dreams will not necessarily become reality.

33

There are two types of dreams you can choose from. There is your vision and illusion. Your vision is what will happen if you use a certain approach and put in some kind of work. Illusions will deceive you into believing in something that will only happen in your imagination and never outside of it. The worst part of an illusion is that if you keep believing in it, your dream, and I mean your life, will end up into a nightmare.

Make sure your dream is a vision and not an illusion. Here is the difference. A vision is a literary dream that will occur in the future, therefore having the ability to foresee an event or occurrence before it happens. It's like the weather forecast, you look at your phone to check tomorrow's weather and the forecast is heavy rain and you get prepared in the morning of the next day for rain and it happens, this is almost what a vision is. The weather channel was able to see in the future and tell you exactly what was going to happen with the weather the next morning. This is how your dream should be. The weather channel did not just predict the next morning's weather out of fantasy. They use proper equipment to study the temperature pattern and the movement of clouds, the speed of the winds, the movement of the earth, and so on to predict the weather. Your vision had to be based on reality. Yes, sometimes we become tired of having expectations of a better situation. So, we become desperate and start entertaining fantasies in our mind or we start dismissing reality. This is when a dream becomes an illusion. An illusion is a distorted reality that appears to be what it is supposed to be but is not. Illusion is when we look at the sun and see it rising in the east and watch it move in front of our eyes towards the west and then sets as darkness takes over. In reality, the sun never moves around the earth. It is the earth that we are on that is on its axis while moving around the sun. But because we are on earth, we are not realizing that we are moving around the sun. Sunsets and sunrises are illusions, yet they look real. But they are a distorted reality.

Here is another example. You are sitting at the window of a train and see the landscape move by you in the opposite direction. This is an illusion. The reality is that it is you who is moving, not the trees or the buildings passing you by.

A person who does not know the science of rotation (a complete spinning of the earth around its axis in 24 hours) and revolution (the movement of the earth around the sun in 365 days), will believe that the sun rises and sets every day.

Whatever your dream is, be realistic and honest with yourself. Don't be in denial of facts in front of you. Do what you can and acknowledge the difficulties in front of you. Come up with the best ideas and solutions to deal with what may be impediments to what you are trying to accomplish. Take responsibility for your actions and do not blame others for what you are not doing right. Acknowledge your mistakes and shortcomings and make corrections and improvements where needs are. It is ok, to have faith in a higher power and to believe in divine providence, or luck. But you have to believe in yourself first. Think about it. Think about it, whoever you believe in as the supreme being or the higher power, will not come and do for you what you are supposed to do for yourself. So, if you spend all your time on your knees and wait for a miracle, instead of doing what you need to do to make things better for yourself, your dream may end up either, either into an illusion or into a nightmare, or simply nowhere.

Always remember that a vision is based on reality and an illusion is based on fantasy. When you are engaging in fantasy instead of being realistic about what you are doing, don't be surprised that you are constantly failing and never succeeding in whatever you are doing.

In my book, Homeless Lives Matter: Homeless My Story, I have discussed with great detail, how I ended up being homeless and what I experienced as a homeless person. So, I am not going to repeat everything in this book. But I decided to write books and sell enough of them to become financially independent as an activist writer. A man that I met on the streets while he was helping the homeless and who I befriended, suggested that I write about my homeless experience. First, I was not interested in doing that, then I thought I should go ahead and do so. Two years later, I self-published a book about my experience as a homeless person. Although I started writing the book in 2016, I finished and self-published it in 2017. Then, I took about 6 months to rest before I decided to sell it on the street.

First, I did not know for sure how I was going to sell it outside. I took a bike ride around the downtown area to locate streets that had a lot of pedestrian traffic not just in the daytime but also in the evening. I settled on the block on F street and E street on 15th street, in the northwest part of town. The White House is two blocks around the corner. The Washington Monument and the African American Museum are also two blocks south of there. The National Mall and all the Museums which are part of the Smithsonian Institution are within walking distance. So, the spot where I sold my book, right in front of Old Ebbitt Grill, Washington DC's oldest Restaurant, was very traveled by tourists visiting the White House and all the tourist attractions on the National Mall. And adjacent to the White House, is the Treasury Department. There are also a lot of federal government agencies and offices in the area. So, in addition to the tourists, there were also a lot of government employees walking past me. Also, Old Ebbitt Grill had a lot of customers, who were dining there or going to the bars inside there. SO, it was an ideal place to sell my books and I did pretty well there. But, not enough to save to get a place as I planned. But I was making enough to feed myself and take care of my basic needs.

Then came the coronavirus epidemic. Governments around the world including here in the US, imposed a shutdown on all public, social and commercial activities and recommended people to stay indoors and only come out when necessary and urgent and do so under social distancing by staying 6 feet apart.

I decided to resort to social media to sell my books because I could no longer do so on the street. I successfully sold enough books online to afford a place.

In February 2021, I was able to use some of the saved money I made selling my book, to rent my own apartment after being homeless for a long time. But this is not the success I was envisioning, but progress towards it. In that sense, myself, the rotten fruit, has turned into a fresh plant. This is progress. But success will be when the plant turns into a tree that will produce fruits. When I was explaining that to that person, I touched the tree I was sitting next too, to show her how a rotten fruit, that is planted in fertile soil, and properly watered can turn into a strong tree that will reproduce more fruits.

I'd rather be a lonely poor homeless bum living in the woods in peace and harmony with nature and getting along with trees, birds, insects, than being around human beings who love drama and being miserable. I just believe that what we should all be longing for are peace and happiness. Otherwise, what is life worth if you have a good job, a roof over your head, a nice car, money in the bank, but want to be unhappy? I am not here to judge anybody, but it is obvious to me that some people just like to be miserable and make everybody around them miserable. I don't know what kind of gratification anyone will feel out of creating unhappiness inside their soul and around them.

I cannot tell you how shameful and sad I have felt about my life as a homeless person. Even talking about it publicly is disgusting, to tell you the truth. I don't feel any pride coming up here and showing you another person's couch or living room where I sleep or kitchen where I cook my meal or a tent in the woods where I sleep. But I can overcome those bad feelings and look at the greater picture, of how sharing my story can inspire and motivate so many of you and also create awareness about Homelessness and the reality of some of us who suffer from it.

But I am still happy to be alive and enjoy the good things and beautiful things in my sad and undesirable predicament. And I want to see everybody happy. So, I don't like to see unhappiness and misery and drama and chaos around me and from people I interact with. Please be happy, don't make yourself miserable, and don't make other people around you miserable. We all deserve peace and happiness. So, I believe.

Believe in yourself.

You can stay on your knees all your life and pray or wish for good luck to change your predicament but waiting on a miracle without taking any action to make things better can disable you and prolong your condition. There is so much you can do for yourself without expecting a miracle except in situations beyond your control. For example, if you get an incurable disease like HIV, there is nothing you can do to cure it, but you can still take care of your medication and do certain things to keep your body in good health and not worsen your condition. What I am trying to tell you is not to give up on hope or stop praying for a miracle. I am just telling you to do your part, while you pray or hope for better. Do not just pray and hope and fold your hands and do nothing and just expect a miracle. You can get lucky, but you may also not.

At least if you pray and wish and do what you have to do, you are maximizing the chances of things getting better.

Other than that, it is all in your hand. Either you are going to figure a way out of your predicament, or you just sit there and get stuck and let things get worse. It is your choice to do something about what you are going through or just give up on yourself and let the situation make your life worse. You cannot get anything accomplished if you don't believe that you can. You have to believe in yourself before you believe in anything else.

Animals get up as soon as the sun rises and get busy doing what they have to do to feed and take care of themselves in an environment that is most of the time very dangerous because they are themselves prey to other animals. One day, I was in my tent sleeping. I opened my eyes and saw a hawk fly low and snatch a small bird that was trying to find something to eat in front of my tent. So, you can just observe animals around you and how they are busy looking for food but protecting themselves at the same time against any potential danger, then you can understand that survival is a reality of every living being. You never see an ant, or a spider, or a fox, or a pigeon, or a raccoon get on their knees and pray or go to a church or a mosque or a temple or any place of worship to ask God to give them food or a place to live. If you ever see one of them in your church or your mosque or your temple, they are only there to look for food or to shelter themselves. They know what they have to do to survive. So should you and I.

When I was homeless and was selling my book, some people walked straight to me, and instead of asking me how much my book cost, they just told me to believe in Jesus and my life will be better. I would use sarcasm to make my point when responding to them. I used to say," I think I will be wasting God's time by praying to him and asking him to do for me what I can do for myself". And I gave them the following example:" Imagine your 8-year-old son asking you to come and wipe his behind after he uses the toilet. I am quite sure you will ignore him because you have trained him to do that when he was younger. I think when we pray and ask God to do for us what we can do for ourselves, there will not be answers just like in the example I just gave.

If you are lazy and want everything free in life and do not want to make any effort to make things better for yourself, you can pray all you want, nothing is going to happen. You cannot just be frustrated about life or your condition and just stay depressed and pray for God to come and do for you want you can do for yourself and expect an answer to your prayer.

You have to believe in yourself because whoever created you equipped you with the tools to deal with difficulties just like he did with other living beings.

By believing in yourself, I simply mean that you have to have self-confidence and feel motivated to do for yourself. If you can't for reasons beyond your control, then it is what it is. Nothing you can do. But in most cases, folks get on their knees and pray for God to do for them for things they can do themselves. No wonder their prayers remain unanswered. I know some of you reading what I am writing believe in God and some of you do not. I will respect both believers and non-believers. So, I am not using these examples as a believer or as a non-believer. I am just making a point by just using logic. My point is this, if you don't have a job and trying to get one, you can pray to God to help you, but you still need to go out there and find a job. When we were younger, we had to go on the job site and feel applications and then be called in for an interview. Today, you have to go online to do that. Another example, if you are sick and pray to God to heal you, you still have to get up and go to the hospital or take your medication to get well. Miracles happen, I am not denying it. But you have to make miracles happen by your attitude and actions.

To believe in yourself means to have confidence in yourself and not feel defeated and hopeless or insecure about your ability to resolve difficult issues you are facing. To believe in yourself is being able to say yes, I can. Yes, I can do my very best to make my life better and deal with my issues better. To talk to yourself like that is a great attitude that will encourage you to do what needs to be done.

I am no longer homeless today after a very long time in that predicament, and that is because I decided one day to be mentally strong and believe in myself and say to myself that, yes, I can do what needs to be done to survive and make it better in the process.

I do not want to repeat what I already wrote extensively in my book, Homeless Lives Matter Homeless My reality. But as I wrote in that book, I took my bike one day and rode up North Capitol Street in Washington DC and found a peaceful quiet wooded area and set up there as my new shelter. I ended up setting a tent there and equipped it with a full-size bed. I made it very comfortable for myself and lived there for about five years.

Was it safe to live in a tent in an area where I was alone and where there were no houses around? Well, I never had any problem there, but it was a dangerous thing to do because anybody could have attacked me in my sleep in that tent in the midst of nowhere without any witness. But, for some reason, I never felt scared to sleep in a tent in the dark under a tree surrounded by bushes and exposed to wild animals. The wild animals were not my concern. What I was afraid of the most, were human beings. An animal will harm you for two reasons, either you are food to them, or you are a danger to them. Other than that, animals will not harm you, human beings will. In Homeless Lives Matter: Homeless My Reality, I recount the story of the kids who tried to set me on fire while I was sleeping in a back-alley's loading duck.

Today, I am no longer homeless. I am selling enough books to move to the next level. Mission accomplished. But I did not just get on my knees and pray or simply wish myself good luck. I had to put in work.

First, I had to find a place to live without having to pay rent since I had no money. I did not want to be in a homeless shelter. I did not want to be living on somebody's floor couch unless I had to because I was either not feeling in good health or was trying to get out of the elements (cold, heat, heavy rain, snow). I wanted to be alone and in a peaceful environment and away from confusion and too many people.

But I set up the tent in an area where I was not very worried about anybody trying to do me harm. The area was located between a hospital, a basilica, and an army soldiers' home (military cemetery). The symbolism of my location was not lost on me. The church (Basilica of the National Shrine of the Immaculate Conception) symbolized to me the spiritual realm of life or reality). I am not a religious person, but I believe that there is a spiritual or invisible or a supernatural, (whichever word you prefer) dimension of life and reality and that we can be affected by that dimension. As far as religion is concerned, I am agnostic, but I respect all beliefs and believe that there is another dimension to life and existence beyond the physical. So, I reach out to that dimension without knowing exactly what it is. So, having a majestic sacred building around me is a great thing as far as I am concerned. I care less if it is a Church, a Mosque, a synagogue, or a temple. It is a sacred building as far as I am concerned. I felt spiritually protected by being close to a sacred house of worship.

The second place around me was the Washington hospital Center complex and particularly the Veteran hospital right on the side of my tent. That was also something that made me feel safe because, in case of illness or accident or attack by humans or animals, I could walk to the Washington Hospital Center emergency room in less than ten minutes.

The third place was the Military cemetery behind me. A cemetery reminds me of the last place our body rested after life is drained from it. The cemetery is also where our soul is supposed to rest in peace. To me, a cemetery is a constant reminder of the fact that we, human beings do not live forever and that while we are still alive, we have to survive to stay alive and live a meaningful life before it is time to go.

Anytime I walk past a cemetery, I stop to remind myself that I am not here forever and that before my time comes, I have to accomplish my purpose and not feel like my experience as a human being on earth was worthless.

It took faith in myself to even go set up a tent under a tree in bushes alone. But I needed that isolation to be able to accomplish my goals. My goal was to write a successful book and sell it and use the money to start my life over again by getting a place to live and starting a business and more.

Raccoon in my tent

Second, I had to make sure I had a comfortable bed to sleep on. What I did was walk down the street, about a quarter of a mile away to Michigan Avenue where the houses started and walk in the alleys to see if I could find any discarded mattresses. I did find a few of them and waited till very late at night, around 2 or 3 am to come and get them and drag them all the way to my tent. I first got a small mattress. But one night, I heard a loud bang while I was sleeping around 2 am. I waited till around 5 am and came out of my tent. There was a big full-size mattress with a memory foam topper on the side of the road but close enough to my tent. Maybe, about 100 feet away. Somebody probably dropped it purposely for me to use. I dragged it to my tent and had a comfortable bed to sleep on from then. I kept a butcher knife and a heavy metal pole inside for protection.

I kept not only my clothes inside but also my computer sometimes. I don't know if it was luck or if it was some kind of supernatural protection, but anytime I came back to my tent, my laptop was always there. Nothing ever disappeared from my tent. I was even stupid enough to forget money in the pocket of a pant sometimes, but it was still there when I came back. The most incredible thing is that sometimes I was in my tent late at night in pitch darkness with only the moon and the stars as light, but I would go to sleep at peace without worrying about getting harmed by animals or human beings.

This was not your normal place to call home, but I had created a temporary home to allow me to have a good sleep inside a covered and spacious enough dwelling where I could keep my belongings. I could also shower outside of it. All I had to do was put my shorts on, get a gallon or two of water, use some soap and body wash, sit in a chair, and shower. Nobody could see me, really. There were almost no pedestrians walking around except one or two the whole day.

The whole thing here is that I had to create some kind of comfort for myself in a hostile environment to survive.

Things may be difficult but make a way for yourself and make it easy on yourself. Always believe that you can make it easier and better and do it.

Be courageous in life if you want to make it. Don't just give up because things are tough. You are to fail if you do not arm yourself with courage and face adversity. Things are not going to be as easy as you expected them. But you have to go through the process and figure a way to jump over or go around the hurdles on your path and keep going ahead. You can't just say, oh no, this is too much, I am not going through this. Things are not just going to happen for you, you have to make it happen.

You have to be persistent. You can't just start something and put it on hold and start it back and put it on hold and start it back and wonder why things are not happening as fast as you desire.

It was a time when I did not have a bike because the bike I had was stolen. I had to either walk from my tent to wherever. When I could, I would catch a bus from downtown to my tent late at night. Sometimes, I will just keep walking until I get to my tent. It was a 40-minute walk. Sometimes, I was so tired but so sleepy, I wanted to get to my tent as soon as possible but my body wanted to stop and rest for a minute and my eyes were about to close. But I used to keep telling myself, the faster you walk the closer you get, and keep walking. "Leo, keep moving. The faster you walk the closer you get, "I kept saying until I got to my tent and jumped on my bed and got into a deep sleep. This became my motto whenever I feel tired and want to stop and get some rest when I know that I am not really far from my destination, and I can get there sooner if I keep moving. I understand that sometimes you are tired and want to pause for a minute. But you are delaying your progress when you stop too often.

You have to be consistent. You can't just start something and then switch up to something else as soon as you realize that the path towards achieving what you started is not going to be as easy as you thought. Unless you realize that what you wanted to accomplish was unrealistic and unachievable as you planned it in the first place, stay the course until you make it.

In my case, I decided to write books, sell them and use the money to get out of the miserable condition that I was in as a homeless person. I never wavered. When I was selling my book Homeless Lives Matter, Homeless My Story outside on the street, a few times, someone approached me and asked me whether I was actually homeless when they saw my signs saying, "Help a homeless self-published author. Get your copy of my book". "Yes" was my answer. "How come you wrote a book and self-published yourself if you are homeless" they kept on. Why can't a homeless person write a book or be an entrepreneur? Don't let other people doubt you discourage you or make you give up or switch up. You know what you can accomplish. So, keep on with what you are doing until you make it.

I already told you to be courageous and persistent. In addition to that, you have to be able to go through the pain and suffering that you may experience while doing what you need to do to make it. I sold my book on the street, under extreme cold weather for hours many times. My fingers and toes were frozen, but I had to endure, which means that I had forced myself to stay outside on the street and sell my book despite the suffering I went through. People seeing me staying in the cold instead of packing and leaving, had more empathy for me and went ahead and bought a copy of my book because they admired my resiliency. Be willing to make sacrifices. Don't expect things to happen that easily for you. Everything is not going to be comfortable or convenient. But you have to endure till you succeed. Believe in yourself.

Chapter 3:

That I have to be aware of reality around me

(Be aware of about issues affecting humanity and the environment and commit for change}

Hard times taught me this lesson. That I must be aware and conscious about what is going on around me and in the world, because everything that is happening as the result of either nature or human actions, affects me, everybody, and everything.

Always remember that you do not exist on this planet earth alone; and that they are an innumerable amount of living beings and other natural elements coexisting on this planet with you. Be aware that everything that is happening on planet earth affects you, and everything you do affects planet earth.

There is something called right and there is something called wrong. And there is something called good and there is something called evil.

Although you may not agree that how you think or act as an individual or as a group may be wrong, or you may not know right from wrong, be aware that there is something called reality and there is something called illusion, which is a distorted reality, sometimes purposely created to deceive and control you and deceive and control humanity. To think that the wrong and evil actions caused by humans, around you or away from you, individually or collectively should be ignored as long as it does not affect you directly, is an illusion. The reality is that you are part of humanity and what is going on in your community, in society, and the world will affect you someway, somehow.

Be aware that although we are of different races, religions, ideologies, political affiliations, gender, social status, all of us humans are only one species, with the same blood color, same humanity, same desire for peace, health, happiness, and prosperity.

Never think that you are better than anybody else. Never look down on others because they are sick, handicapped, mentally ill, physically unattractive to you, obese, skinny, blind, deaf, gay, old, lonely, or homeless. All of us are in this world facing the same aspirations for a better life and the same desire to be treated with dignity.

I like to be happy no matter what I go through. Everything that causes me and other human beings' unhappiness and suffering, is of concern to me, particularly issues regarding poverty, human dignity, human rights, and the environment. Because I experienced homelessness chronically, the issue of homelessness is what I chose to be an advocate of. I started my homeless activism by writing and self-publishing the book Homeless Lives Matter, Homeless My Story. Here is the introduction to the book on the back cover. Actually, this is an edited version that I posted on the website of Amazon.

Thousands of men and women in Washington DC, as elsewhere in mostly urban but also parts of rural America, are severely afflicted by abject poverty and not able to earn enough to take care of their daily needs, basically food and a place to call home. Every night the homeless, as they are called, sleep outside on street sidewalks and corners, under bridges, on sides of buildings, in bushes, on public benches, in train and bus stations, and anywhere else where they can find a place to sleep at least for a night. Although this reality of total destitution in the midst of abundance occurs in the greatest, mightiest and wealthiest nation on earth, the issue of homelessness is generally met by apathy, probably because most people who walk past the homeless every day seem unable to relate to what it is like to be homeless. In order to awaken the consciousness of the reader and the general public about this social plague called homelessness, the author is telling his story as a homeless himself and portraying the reality of homelessness from his experience. His message is simple: Homelessness is dehumanizing and detrimental to the individual experiencing it. Homelessness should alarm society as a whole because it has reached an epidemic proportion that is afflicting and incapacitating a considerable and non-negligible segment of the American population. There should therefore be urgency, from individuals and society to act to solve and end homelessness, so that human dignity can be restored in the lives of so many human beings who have no home and dwell outside like animals in the wilderness. Also, so many who are socially and financially stable and self-sufficient, or are just doing well enough, think that they are immune to homelessness and poverty. The truth of the matter is that they may be mistaken because they cannot predict any affliction or misfortune that can cause them to lose everything and become indigent themselves.

In one of the stories in the book, I had explained how the women at SOME were asked to stay outside in the cold or the heat, from 6 am when men were allowed in the seating area while breakfast was prepared and before everybody was allowed in the dining area at 7 am. A year after I wrote the book, I was in the dining room waiting to take a shower. A staff lady from the SOME office was walking between the entrance door to the dining room door and stopping by the door leading to the showers. I went to check on the shower list to see how far I had to wait. She saw me coming from the showers area. "Can I ask you a few questions for my survey?" She asked me. "Yes," I said to her. Then she asked me questions about how satisfied I was with the showers. I looked at her and asked her to follow me outside because I wanted to show her something related to the showers. When we got outside, I told her to look at these women waiting outside for the dining room to be open for breakfast while a man was waiting in the waiting room inside. It was cold outside. Not freezing but chilly, nonetheless. The reason why women were asked to wait outside was that men's showers were taking place from 6 am to 8:30 am and women's showers from 9:30 to 11pm. The reality of it is that there was a door to the

49

entrance of the shower room and even if the door was open, nobody in the waiting room was able to see inside the shower area. So, to keep the women outside in the cold when it was freezing in the winter or the heat when it was 100 degrees outside, did not make sense to me. When I explained all that to the lady, she agreed with me. She even pulled on her jacket by stating that although she had a jacket on her, she still felt cold outside. We were standing by the women in line outside the door. "What you think we should do to solve this problem?" I think you should let the women in and maybe have the door to the shower room closed, or just put a curtain up. She thanked me for bringing this situation to her attention and promised that she will bring it to the attention of her supervisors. The next day, I saw her continuing her survey. I pulled a copy of my book that I promised her and handed it to her for free. She wanted to give me the book back after she read it, but I told her to keep it. A couple of months later, I went to take a shower at SOME. I noticed that the women were no longer asked to wait outside. They were let in the waiting room with the men when the doors opened at 6:00 am. I am not going to take credit for the changes, but I am glad I was able to express my concern to that staff lady and also talk about it in my book Homeless Lives Matter, Homeless My story.

Now that I am no longer homeless, at least for now, I intend to be more involved on the street as an activist for the homeless. But here are some of the actions I undertook as a homeless advocate while I was still homeless:

One afternoon, in the spring of 2018, I decided to go get myself some coffee at McDonald's on 13th and New York Avenue, Northwest, Washington DC. It was around 7 pm. I was just taking a break since I had been selling my book on the street, a few blocks away on 15th Street since early afternoon, and was planning to keep selling books until 10 pm. It was a little cold outside. When I entered McDonald's, there were about three customers in front of me. Two regular guys, and, at the counter, in front of him, there was a guy with a wool blanket on his shoulders. That clearly showed that he was a homeless guy. When the line moved up, the homeless guy who was about my age, fiftyish, and whom I knew on the street, walked to me while the lady at the counter was taking the order of the guy before him. "Do you have a dollar and ten cents?" he said to me while holding a twenty-dollar bill in his hand. As I was reaching in my pocket to try to get a dollar and ten cents, I got curious to know why he needed a dollar and 10 cents when he had a twenty-dollar bill in his hand. "I am trying to get a cup of coffee, but she doesn't wanna take the twenty-dollar bill. She says she ain't got no change."

"Bullshit", I responded while putting my money back in my pocket. "She has changed. Get back in line, and tell her that, this is all you got. She can't refuse to serve you because you only have a twenty-dollar bill. This doesn't make any sense." I responded while making some space in front of me and the customer at the counter. When he told her that he could not get some change, she asked him to order more food for her to take his order. He told her that he only wanted some coffee. She reluctantly took the twenty-dollar bill and took his order for a $1.10 coffee and opened a drawer and had no problem getting him the right change. I was homeless and looked homeless because of my untidy appearance. I was carrying my big backpack on my back also. I had a lot of dollar bills and coins in my pocket. I only wanted a coffee also. It cost $1.10. But I decided to try that lady and see if she would treat me the same way as she treated the homeless man in front of me. I am quite convinced that she would have not refused to take the order of a regular non-homeless person who only had a twenty-dollar bill and wanted to order some coffee.

"Can I take your order?" She said to me, "Yes, mam, one large cup of coffee". I said back to her. "Anything else?" she asked. "No, that's all," I responded. "One dollar twenty cents," she said. "No, no, no, I don't have any change. You got to order more food" she raged when I handed a twenty-dollar bill. I told her that that was all I had. She told me she had no change and that I should order more food for her to take my order. I told her that I only wanted some coffee. She then ignored me and took the order of the customer behind me. I insisted that she takes my order. She paid me no mind. I asked for her manager. At that point, the security officer, walked up to me and asked me what the problem was. I explained to her. After I did, she pointed to a sign on the entrance wall to indicate to me that the store has the right to refuse to serve anyone. I told her that, in that case, I would complain to whoever was the boss above the manager running that store because I would consider such a denial of service, discrimination and I would put it on social media to tell the whole world about it. The security guard then told me that I couldn't film inside the store and that is probably because I am filming the employee that she refused to serve me. I told her that it was bogus. She refused to serve me because she does not want to accept my order of a $1 coffee since I was not ordering more food for my twenty-dollar bill. The security guard walked away.

The manager was standing next to the cashier. "What is the problem?" she asked me. I explained that her co-worker refused to take my order. Both spoke to the manager, who then went by her business and ignored me. I pulled my phone out again and told the manager that I would record the incident and put it on social media to show the world how McDonald's treats certain customers. At that point, the manager said something to the lady. And the lady went ahead and took my twenty-dollar bill and served me. I put my phone back in my pocket and waited for my coffee. When I grabbed the coffee that the cashier lady just sat on the counter instead of handing to me as she does with other customers, the security guard called me by the soda fountain area. "You can't come here anymore after today," she said to me. "I will come back here anytime I want to. You don't own this store and you can't prevent me from coming here". And she kept following me while I was exiting the store. As soon as I stepped out of the door, she pulled her phone to take a facial picture of me. I pulled out my phone also and tried to take her picture, but she turned back and went inside the store.

I reported the incident by email to McDonald's customer service office. I went by my business and forgot about the whole situation until another incident happened at the same McDonald's, four months later with another cashier. She also refused to serve me because of an incident that I reported earlier. I sent another email again to McDonald's customer service office to complain about this third incident.

Here is the answer I received.

From: McDonald's Response <donotreply@csmcd.net>

Sent: Tuesday, September 11, 2018, 12:02:38 PM

To: leognawa@hotmail.com

Subject: McDonald's Response

Hello Mr. Gnawa:

Thank you for taking the time to share your recent experience at the McDonald's located at 1235 New York Ave NW. As the Customer Service Representative of this restaurant, I hope you will accept my apology for your unsatisfactory visit. I called your contact number twice to speak with you personally, but I was not successful in reaching you.

Our goal is 100-percent customer satisfaction, and my team works hard to deliver fast, friendly, and accurate service to guarantee that each visit you make is a pleasant one. I'm sorry you feel we have let you down. Please be assured, I am following up at my restaurant to address this issue.

Your e-mail serves as a valuable reminder that our customers are our number one priority. We truly appreciate your feedback and again thank you for taking the time to share your experience with us. We hope to have the opportunity to serve you in the future.

Jessie Morrell

McDonald's Customer Service Representative

New York Ave

(703) XXX.XXXX

I never answered that email although I was satisfied that someone at McDonald's took the time to respond and offer me an apology. To me, this was a resolved issue until I went back there a couple of months later and got denied service by the same Hispanic cashier. On Monday, January 10, 2019, I emailed the customer service representative to complain again.

From: Leo gnawa <leognawa@hotmail.com>

Sent: Thursday, January 10, 2019, 3:33:31 PM

To: ----@fecmanagement.net

Subject: Re: McDonald's Response

To Jessie Morrell,

I am reaching back to you because of a new situation that occurred at the same location, where I was again denied service on Monday, January 7th, 2019 by a manager in the store.

I did record most of the incident on my phone and am willing to show it to you before posting it on YouTube. But first, let me wish you a happy New Year 2019 and thank you for responding to my last complaint.

Unfortunately, there seems to be a serious systematic problem in that store that needs to be addressed and corrected. I am, therefore, really sending this email so that this type of discrimination and denial of services to some people because of their race and social status, ceases.

As a homeless activist and self-published author (Homeless Lives Matter, on amazon), I do advocate for the respect of the dignity of people afflicted by homelessness and do write about mistreatments and abuses of homeless people. This explains why I take this complaint to heart because I think this is a case exposing the denial of service and discrimination of people who may look like me.

Here is what happened. On Saturday, January 5th, 2019, my friend Lisa called me and asked me to buy her a salad at McDonald's. I told her to meet me there at about 2 pm. Once there we locked out bikes outside and went inside to place orders. I was hungry so I decided that we eat inside. But the dining room downstairs was crowded. I thought about eating upstairs, but there was a trash structure blocking the stairs. I assumed the upstairs dining room was not open. But as my friend and I were following the manager to the area of the store where iced beverages were made. She called an old worker who was mopping the floor in proximity. I heard her speak to him, and point at a person holding his tray. The old worker walked up to the man and spoke to him, then walked him to the stairs, moved the trash structure, and led him upstairs. At that point, I understood that they were selectively choosing who they wanted to use in the upstairs room. I whispered to my friend what I had just witnessed and told her that, we should go sit upstairs as well. Though we were still waiting for our order, I decided to go reserve us a table upstairs by the window and come back to help her carry the food upstairs. But as I got to the trash structure that was blocking the stairs in order to make a way, the old worker who was standing nearby, rushed to me and told me that the upstairs was closed. I told him that I had just seen him taking a customer up there. Then he responded that, it was because that customer had purchased some food. I told him that I am also a customer, and I purchased some food also. He asked me to show him my food. At that point I responded that I did not feel that I had to show him anything unless he was willing to reimburse me the money I spent for my food. At that point he moved the trash structure back to block the path, but I move it back out of my way and told him he that was wrong to only allow white folks upstairs. I went upstairs, chose a table and took my jacket off and freed my hands since I had a backpack. I came back downstairs to help my friend with the food, and we went to eat upstairs where there were about 5 customers, all of them were whites. Though I was saddened by what happened, I left the store after we finished eating and did not make much of it. But on Monday evening, as I decided to take a break from my activities and go get a coffee at McDonald's, I noticed a white person upstairs at I locked my bike on the side of 13th Street. When I got inside the store, I ordered a large coffee from a young friendly lady behind the counter. As she took my order, I asked her if the dining room upstairs was open. I noticed that the trash structure was blocking the stairs again and the same lady manager was running the store. The cashier lady hesitated to give me an answer. She turned to the manager and spoke to her. The manager then told me that the dining room upstairs was closed. I asked her what time they closed. She said "6:30 pm". I told but it is only 6:09 pm and that from outside, I have seen a white customer upstairs. She responded that those upstairs were the last customers allowed upstairs. At that point, it was clear to me that she was not allowing homeless folks up there, even if they were customers and wanted to go eat their meal upstairs. I told the lady that if I could not sit and drink my coffee in the store, it was no point of me spending my money there, and I stepped out. But as soon as I got outside, I decided to come back and document the incident by recording it on my phone as evidence. So, I went back to the counter in front of the manager and ordered a large coffee. Then asked her why she told me that the upstairs was closed while it was not 6:30 and therefore not allowing me to use the dining room up there. When she noticed that I was recording it on my phone, she asked me if I was recording it, I told her yes because I wanted to make sure I had a record of the incident. At that point, she changed the whole story and started making fabrications. She said that I go upstairs to sleep all the time. What she said, was so ridiculous because I do not come to that McDonald often, and when I do, I rarely consume my order in there. And when I do, it is for a very brief moment. I had no need to stay at that McDonald's for no longer than the time I need to buy a meal or consume it if I decided to do so inside. Then she kept on with the lies, such as, I leave my belongings upstairs. I was shocked that she will just

56

make up anything to justify what she really does in that store, as far as denying equal access services to black and homeless folks, although she happens to be black herself.

Sorry if this complaint was long, but I hope this issue is addressed and that I and other people looking like me can be served and be allowed to consume our purchased items at any dining room inside the store like anybody else.

My phone number is (202) XXX XXXX

Sincerely,

Leo Gnawa

I received a call the next day from Jessie Morrell, the McDonald's customer service representative. She asked me if I was willing to meet the McDonald District Manager for the area and the Store Manager together? I agreed and met both at the date that the customer service representative set.

A couple of days later, I went to the meeting a little before noon at the same McDonald's to meet with both the district manager and the Store Manager. They invited me upstairs. As we got up the stairs together and sat at the table set in the corner, the manager spotted a homeless man sleeping in a chair and leaning on a table not far from us. There were customers up there. She woke up the homeless man and told him to leave. He grabbed his stuff and left right away. Both managers went ahead and explained to me that they had problems with homeless people using the upstairs to sleep as we had just witnessed. I explained to her that it was fair for the store employees to not allow anybody including the homeless to sleep upstairs. But it was unfair for them to assume that anyone who looks homeless or who is homeless, would go upstairs to sleep. But they kept insisting that the homeless were a problem for their customers. To argue her case, the manager said that the store had a lot of tourists as customers because it was located a few blocks from the White House and that they were concerned about their safety, the reason why they had to keep the homeless away. I was very shocked to hear that these managers viewed the homeless as a problem instead of an asset.

This is why I kept saying at the beginning of this chapter that you have to be aware. Obviously, these managers of McDonald's lack awareness of the value of the homeless for their business. They looked down on their most valuable customers because they were poor homeless people, to cater to folks who look normal, regular, and have more money. I told her that the dollar bill of a homeless man and homeless woman holds the same value as the dollar of a tourist from out of town. And I went further to make my point. I told them that the homeless men and women who were hanging around the area and who to them were a problem were more reliable, consistent, and regular customers than the tourists on their way to visit or from visiting the White House, who stopped and consumed there once in their life before returning to California, New York, Florida, Canada, Japan, Germany, England, Sweden, France, Australia or wherever. The homeless man and woman come back and forth inside the store to spend all day, on coffee or sandwiches, the money they make all day by begging outside. Do you know how much money you guys make from the homeless who spend their money here all day long while the tourists are gone? The store was staying open 24 hours. So, they had homeless customers 24 hours including hours when no tourists were around and when they had low traffic. At the end of the conversation, they agreed with me that their employees should treat the homeless better and not refuse to serve them. They agree to take my suggestions into account and treat the homeless as regular customers and not as undesirable customers. I left around 2:00 pm after our two-hour meeting and went back to 15th Street to sell my book on the street.

Never look down on others because they are sick, handicapped, mentally ill, physically unattractive to you, obese, skinny, blind, deaf, gay, old, lonely, or just different. All of us are in this world facing the same aspirations for a better life.

58

We all go to the toilet and the wealthy man's feces don't smell as good as the expensive cologne he wears. Trust me, Jeff Bezos, Elon Musk, Bernard Arnault, Bill Gates, Mark Zuckerberg, and Warren Buffet's shit smells just as bad as the shit of the dirty homeless bum sleeping under the bridge. We are all the same. Let's remind ourselves of that. And then we will see ourselves in others and treat them as we want to be treated.

All the troubles in the world including homelessness, hatred, cruelty, apathy, intolerance, racism, police brutality, and all forms of inhumanity towards our fellow human beings are because we don't see other humans as the same as us.

I don't like to see people be mean to others. We are all here together and we are all going to die one day and be gone. So, while we are still here let's treat others with respect and dignity.

To me, the cure for all this evil and apathy is to just realize that we have a common humanity and the same essence. You may have a different ideology, beliefs, religion, opinion, culture, racial identity, social condition, and political affiliation than somebody else, but as I said in the beginning, we are all members of the human species, and we are all impacted by whatever happens within humanity and the world. You should therefore be aware and support efforts to end the inhumanity of humans towards humans so that we can all live in a world that is better for itself, and better for us, and future generations after us.

When it comes to very controversial issues, I choose to be in the center ideologically speaking and look at both sides of the issue in all fairness and see what makes sense and what does not, from my perspective. I cannot tell you not to have a radical opinion on any issue if you are convinced that your opinion is the right opinion. I am only suggesting that you open your mind and listen to the other side and decide whether some of what they are advocating is making sense or not to you. But avoid being extremist when it comes to your opinion. To be extremist to me is to be close-minded and not trying to understand the other side of the issue. The extremist attitude only breeds intolerance and hatred. Nobody is ever right hundred percent.

Make sure that what you are advocating for or agreeing with, does not serve the selfish interest of only your side or your group to the detriment of others. We may disagree on a lot of things, but there is always something we can commonly agree on. Always seek that common ground so that our differences and diverging opinions will not turn us into enemies or give us the perception that those who disagree with us are our enemies.

Let us fight for what is right for humanity as a whole and not only for our individual and group interests only.

In recent years, we have seen the rise of police brutality against black men and women, and children all over the United States.

Although it was created by black activists, the Black Lives Matter movement attracted and was supported by millions of folks of all races but in the majority young white males and females who paralyzed the streets of major US cities to demand justice for the victims and an end to the killing of blacks by the police.

I was in front of the White House so many times, participating in Black Lives Matter Protest, and was elated to see the diversity of protesters, Blacks, Whites, Asians, Hispanics. It was so beautiful to see.

On April 20, 2021, Officer Derrick Chauvin was found guilty of second-degree unintentional murder, third-degree murder, and second-degree manslaughter for killing a black man, George Floyd in Minneapolis. The Killing of George Floyd created a greater rage and exasperation that made protests bigger and more widespread. Millions invaded public places in different states at the same time. Roads, malls, and other public areas were occupied by thousands of protesters who demanded justice for George

Floyd and police reform. The conviction and guilty verdict of Derrick Chauvin shows that when human beings put their racial identity on the side and see others as humans like them and stand together against injustice, justice is more likely to happen.

I started this chapter by asking you to pay attention to what is going on around you. Because it happened to somebody else does not mean that it may never happen to you. You have to be conscious that fighting for somebody else is also fighting for you.

What happened to George Floyd, and the rest of the black victims of white police officers almost happened to me. I was fortunate enough that I did not end up getting killed for no reason by a police officer who seemed to be looking for someone to be his victim.

I had just left the Safeway on New York and 5th street Northwest. It was open until midnight. It normally stays open 24 hours, until the coronavirus pandemic caused restrictions to be imposed and people to be ordered to stay indoors and only come out to shop for food and other essential needs. I stayed in my tent all day and came out late at night to get what I needed at the Safeway. It was hard to find bread and water because people used to buy as many of those commodities as they could. I was lucky enough to get about three one-gallon bottles of water. I could not find any bread. But I already had some crackers and tuna cans in my tent. So, water was basically the most important item that I needed.

After I got my stuff, I rode my bike up on New York Avenue until I passed New Jersey Avenue. When I was approaching 1st Street, I got off my bike to take a break from pedaling uphill. I had a long way to go and most of my trajectory, on North Capitol Street, was uphill all the way to my tent. It was probably around midnight. I decided to cross the street and get back on my bike and ride up on New York Avenue and turn left on North Capitol Street till Florida Avenue and get off again and walk up to Rhode Island Avenue, then keep on riding on North Capitol until I get tired and stop again. The street was dead empty. There was barely any soul out there. Most people were in self-quarantine because of the pandemic. As I was about to cross the street, I saw a car coming on my left side. I waited till that car passed me. Then I saw another car coming. It was a police car with flashlights on but no siren sound. He was driving fast. He passed me and went to the red light a good block away on North Capitol Street. I started crossing the street when I saw him speeding back in reverse towards me while I was almost in the middle of the road. He turned his light in my face and said to me, "I've seen you breaking into a car not long ago", "No, you did not see me breaking into any car. "I said back. "Yes, I did. I know you, you're always breaking into cars around here. I have a family living on this street block. If one of them ever tells me that their car has been broken into, I will find you." He continued. At that time, I started thinking of the black guys that were killed by police in North Carolina and Florida not long before then. I felt like that officer was trying to find an excuse to shoot me. At that very moment, I felt so powerless and in great danger. My first reaction was to get to my phone and either call 911 or record him. But he kept looking at me menacingly and kept making threats. Then he held his collar and said, "You know you are being recorded right?" "Good, because your camera will not show me breaking any car. And also, there are cameras all over this place, so you know that what you are saying ain't true" I said to him. I felt like he was trying to provoke me and have me say or do something that will be his excuse to shoot me. I asked him to call another officer because I was not feeling safe. He refused. " I am calling 911," I told him as I pulled my phone out of my pocket. He then turns around and sped away. I was trying to turn my camera on and take a videotape of his vehicle, but he was already far away. I dialed 911 and called for help. I explained to the lady who answered the call that I was very scared that this officer threatened me and falsely accused me of breaking into a car. I told her that because of the recent police shooting of innocent black people, I was afraid for my life. I still had to ride up a dark and empty street to my tent in the woods. I don't know if that officer was going to follow me and hurt me. I was seriously afraid. The 911 lady told me that she understood my fear and that she wanted me to stay on the line until an officer showed up. A white lady officer showed up in no time. I dialed the phone of one of the guys that I met on the street and has been checking on me and helping me at times. I apologized to him for waking him up. But he was glad I called him. I wanted a witness while I talked to the second officer. She asked me to describe the officer's car. I did. She told me that it is probably an officer who traveled through the area, and it was not an officer working the area with her. So, there was nothing else she could do. My friend stayed on the line to make sure I was safe while riding to my tent. I told him that I was all right and he could go back to sleep. I rode slowly and kept watching my back to make sure that the first officer didn't follow me. I turn into alleys to avoid riding straight up to my tent. I got to my tent safely and went to sleep.

 Despite that incident, I still believe that there are good police officers out there and that all of them are not out there trying to kill a black person.

But I believe that there should be police reform and that the rallies and marches against police brutality are necessary to end police brutality and especially the killing of black men and women by white police officers.

If you have marched or protested against police brutality and the killing of innocent black men and women, you should be proud of yourself. Let's stand for the respect of human life and human dignity and let's end racism. I will end with these words of wisdom spoken at the United Nations General Assembly on October 4, 1963, by the then Emperor of Ethiopia, His Majesty Haile Selassie I, and made famous by Jamaican Reggae Singer, Bob Marley in his song war:

That until the philosophy which holds one race superior and another inferior

 is finally and permanently discredited and abandoned;

that until there are no longer first-class and second-class citizens of any nation;

that until the color of a man's skin is of no more significance than the color of his eyes;

that until the basic human rights are equally guaranteed to all without regard to race;

that until that day, the dream of lasting peace and world citizenship and the rule of international morality will remain but a fleeting illusion, to be pursued but never attained.

CHAPTER 4

That I have to have empathy

One of the lessons, I have learned in life and through hard times is that I have to be good and kind to other human beings, treat them with compassion and respect their dignity.

I purpose myself to be happy and make others happy otherwise, life is misery. Even when I do not have much, I still give whatever I can to others in need because I see myself in them.

If I had all the gold and diamonds of the world and everybody around me was poor, I would feel miserable and unhappy. Any time I have an opportunity to give, I do not hesitate.

Every day, I give some money to somebody homeless whether it is a dollar or ten dollars. Whatever and whenever I can, I do not hesitate to help somebody out. I really do not like to talk about who I help, so I will not go into further details. But I just want you to know that I was homeless and still giving money to other homeless. So, how much of a loss giving a dollar per day to a homeless man or woman going to be to you?

Do not give only because you expect to get it back or get something in return. Give even when you will never get it back. I can tell that I never give with the expectation to receive back, but the universe always blessed me back.

One day a guy stopped by my book and seemed so interested in my entrepreneurial venture as a homeless. He was a successful businessman and an owner of a factory in South East Asia, precisely, Indonesia if my memory serves me right. I was a little bothered by the fact that he did not buy a copy but was spending too much time trying to teach me a whole business course and tell me how to run mine. I felt I distracted by him because I could not focus on trying to get some to attract customers among the dozens of folks walking by us.

One of the things he was telling me was that when people who come to me had less than the ten dollars I was asking for a copy, I should just give them the copy. In my mind, I was like, "ok, I am here trying to make a profit off selling a copy, so how dumb does that sound? I might as well just give the copies away if I have to take every short money. But actually, I did take a lot of short money and rarely turned anybody down before meeting this guy. I just did not volunteer to give the book out for less or for free, when people asked the price and just left because they did not have enough. In some cases, I asked them how much they had, and still gave the book out when they did not have enough. As I already said, I even gave a copy to folks who did not have the money on them and jokingly told them that they had till next year to pay me. But if they did not have my money by next year, they were still good. "Don't worry about paying me, you good", I use to add after the joke. I just was bothered that the man was trying to tell me things that I already was doing whenever I felt like it. I was not giving the copy, right away to everybody who came with short money because I know some people could afford the book, but were simply trying to be cheap. Some people came out of the bar or restaurant at Old Ebbitt's Grilled where they spent a lot of money on food and drinks. I know they could afford to buy a book from a homeless for ten dollars. "I only got 5 dollars on me" was not something I was accepting all the time from guys who could just go to the most machine inside the restaurant and withdraw enough to get a copy of my book. A few times, people would come and offer me five dollars for a copy. When I told them that the copy was ten dollars, they would exclaim, "ten dollars? That is too much". I felt offended by anybody telling me that 10 dollars were too much for a book that I self-publish and have to buy myself and come to sell on the street. My profit margin was a bit over six dollars. I explained to them that if I was going to sell the book for 5 dollars, I would barely make one dollar as profit. Some of them understood and went into their pockets and pulled a twenty-dollar bill and even asked me to keep the change. Some of them did have only five dollars cash on them. They told me that they will go to the most machine and get more money. Some of them did come back, others did not.

Because of the experience I had with different behaviors from people telling me they only had five dollars, I was using my best judgment to decide who to trust or not and who to give the copy for five dollars or not.

While I was talking to him, someone stopped and told me that they only had four dollars for a copy. "Take it, take it" the man yelled at me. I went ahead and did it.

One day, a family walked by me, the man was black, the wife was white, and the kids were mixed. There were young. Maybe 10 and 7. They stopped, picked a copy, look at it, and walked away. Both kids run back to me and handed me a dollar bill. Thank you I thanked them. Then both picked up a copy each. Before they run back to their parents waiting for them, a quarter of a block away, I said, "I am selling them". They put the copies back down. But I felt terrible and told them that they could have the copies. I felt bad for refusing the copies to some kids who were kind enough to give me a dollar. Why couldn't I give them two copies or at least one, as a gift even if they had no money? From time to time, some folks would hand me a twenty-dollar bill for a copy and asked me to keep the change. I was selling the book for ten dollars on the street.

So when the kids walked back to their parents with the free copies, both kids run back towards me and handed me a hundred-dollar bill. They told me that their parents told me to keep it. I thanked the parents who came back and took a picture with me and the kids holding their copies.

I will admit, I always thought of that businessman when folks come to me and have no money or less than the cost of the book. I hear that man's voice telling me "Never refuse when they have less than ten dollars, always take it".

When folks who have no money but wanted the book refused the copy that I gave them for free, I persuade them to take it by telling them that the copy is already paid for. Indeed, many times, some folks handed me a twenty-dollar bill and asked me to keep the change. In many cases some people even gave me more money, sometimes people gave me fifty or hundred-dollar bills and asked me to keep the change. Others just gave me more money than ten dollars. There were also instances when people talked to me and gave me ten dollars or more and told me to give the book to somebody else because they were going to a bar, or a club, or a show and did not want to be encumbered with the copy in their hands.

This is why I gave so many copies away to many who had no money or less than ten dollars.

I can tell you for sure that I gave a lot and received a whole lot more. What you give out is never lost. It always comes back some way, somehow.

One night, a guy came out of the bar, back and forth to smoke a cigarette not far from me while looking at my signs and me every time. I was hoping that at some point he would approach me and get a copy, but that was not happening. The fourth or fifth time that he came out to smoke a cigarette, he finally stepped towards me. "What are you selling?" He asked me. I went ahead and explained to him that I was a homeless guy who self-published a book to create awareness about homelessness and use the money to get a place one day. " He did not say much. He pulled a fifty-dollar bill out of his pocket and handed it to me and said "You know what? I have been wasting a lot of money drinking all evening. I am having a lot on my mind and I am not happy. But I am just wasting my money because I still have to deal with the issues bothering me. I'd rather you have this fifty-dollar bill than me going back to waste it in the bar". I was very sad and did not feel right taking that money while knowing that the man was going through some tough times. I took the money and tried to talk to him, but he did not reveal much of what issue he was dealing with. I nonetheless found words of encouragement for him and wished him well. He appreciated my compassionate words and left by asking me to pray for him. He was very drunk but did not seem discombobulated.

Anytime I was in need, I desired that someone will come out of nowhere and help me. It was a time when it was very hot outside and I was thirsty and wanted a cold beverage but did not have any money to afford any.

In those days, sodas cans used to cost 50 cents from the soda machine in front of Giant stores and over grocery stores. You can imagine how sad it is when you are thirsty to death, homeless, and don't even have 50 cents to get a soda can.

I remember walking down the street at night and looking on the ground and hoping that I find some money.

But since I started giving a lot, after making more money selling my book, of course, I received more. I am not telling you to give away the little money you have and found yourself without. I am just sharing my experience with you. If you don't have much, make sure you take care of yourself with the little bit you have. I gave a lot because I had my book to fall back on. When I did not have any money, I still could go sell a few copies and have something. You have to give to others but you have to make sure you have enough for yourself.

I received a whole lot from strangers and folks who became what I call my angels. I use the word Angel here figuratively to mean anybody who appears on my path to help and assist me benevolently when I needed help urgently and received it unexpectedly with no ulterior motive from them and for no gain to them.

One day, I was on my way to selling my book. I was on foot because I had a flat tire on my bike. While I was heading to the Safeway store door, a man who had just left the store and was walking towards me, turned back around and started following behind me after he had just passed me. I felt his presence behind me and was very annoyed. I turned around and he immediately told me, "Sorry can I ask you a question?" He said. I had my big bag full of books on my back. "Are you homeless?" He added. "Yes sir". I responded. "Are you homeless for real?" he continued. "Yes, I am, I live in a tent, and actually, I am a self-published author and am going to sell my book titled Homeless Lives Matter. "You want a copy?" I said to him while taking the bag off my back. "No, no, I just want to help you." He said while handing me a $100 bill." "Give the book to somebody else," he said while I was trying to pull a copy out and hand it to him. He then turned and walked back in his initial direction.

One afternoon, I had just got in front of Old Ebbitt's Grill. One of the homeless guys shining shoes in front told me that a white lady came by with signs that she made for me. She promised to come back, he said. I had no idea who that was. I used to sell my books with signs I made myself with cardboard and markers that I used to write the following message on one side of each carb board "Help self-published author. Get your copy of my book. "The signs were ok, but at night the message on them was hardly visible. A few hours later, she came back with professionally made signs from Staples. The messages on the signs were a bit different from the message on my signs. She decided to redo them to my liking. She spent more money getting more signs made with the message that I had on my handmade signs. I picked the new signs myself at Staples when they were made and ready. Since I used the signs she made, I attracted more customers and made more money. My signs and what was written on them could be seen from a distance. The same lady has helped me so many times since. At one point she allowed me to order my orders to her office. All I had to do is show up in front of her office building and she brought the boxes to me when the books came. If she was not in her office, she had her secretary bring them to me downstairs. Her office was half a block from the White House and right around the corner from where I used to sell my book.

She even purchased the last tent I had. She ordered it from the manufacturer in Canada. It was a great tent. In the winter that followed, she brought me an Eddie Bauer jacket. The price tag was still on it. It was around $600. I wore that jacket maybe three times since I had it. She gave it to me two years ago. I gave it to a friend who had his place to keep it for me. The jacket is still in my friend's closet. I felt like folks who see me wearing the jacket while I was selling my book, would wonder why a homeless man wears such an expensive jacket. She bought it for me because it was of great quality and a very warm jacket. But, I had to take into account the mentality of many folks who have a stereotypical image of the homeless.

If I try to list every act of charity and generosity that I have received from strangers while I was in dire need, I will have to write another book especially for that.

I know you cannot help everybody. But I know you can help somebody. You may come across 10 beggars on your path, but even if you cannot give to all of them, give to at least one.

If you can, always help somebody else in need because you never know, you can one day be that somebody else in need of help. Am I right or wrong?

Put yourself in the shoes of others who are going through hard times and are doing worse than you. Imagine that you were homeless or destitute and abandoned by your relatives and friends, and you were out there on the cold or extremely hot streets, begging for money, how would you like passers-by to respond to you? How you think you will feel if hundreds of people walk by you and pay you no mind as if you were invisible. I am quite sure you will feel hurt. So, how you think folks in those situations feel when you just look down on them because of their condition? We always think that bad things always happen to others until we are afflicted with something terrible, then we want everybody else to feel sorry for us. But we were apathetic to others when we were doing fine and never experienced their issues.

I know you know people who care nothing about anybody but their only selves. Do not be like that. If you are, I think you should care about other people because you never know when you are going to need some help from other people. I am just being real with you.

If you don't care to help somebody, do not prevent others to do so. Do not stop anybody's blessings. I already said it. I believe that whatever good you do, it will come back to you someway, somehow. Whatever evil you do also. Nothing is lost in the universe, remember that.

I was selling my book in front of Old Ebbitt Grills, as usual, one evening. A family of tourists came out of the restaurant and stopped in front of my books in the middle of the crowd. There was a man, a woman, some kids, and a young lady who seemed like a visitor in that family. It looked like everybody spoke English pretty well but it appeared that she was visiting from overseas and did not speak English. She pulled a twenty-dollar bill and hand it to me. The man said something to her in French while stopping her from giving me the money. As they were walking away, I called the lady and offered her a free copy of my book. Then the whole family looked back and everybody said thank you to me. The man walked back to me and handed me a five-dollar bill. I kindly refused it. He insisted that I take it for the copy I gave the lady. I told him that it was a gift to her and that I didn't want anything for it. He dropped the money on the copies of my book that were laid on a cardboard box and then walked away. I took the five-dollar bill and threw it on the grass around the tree next to which I was sitting. Half an hour later, a homeless man walked by and I told him that he could have that five-dollar bill.

Do not try to humiliate, embarrass or look down on those you are helping.

I was selling my books on the street as usual. A couple who left the restaurant came in front of me with left-overs in a box and just sat them in front of me without saying anything to me. "I don't want it, take it back please", I told them. They were surprised that I reacted like that. They just picked it back up and walked off. As they walked away, I said to them, I am not an animal. I am a human being like you. You could have handed me the food instead of just sitting it on the ground like you were feeding an animal. I am a human being like you". Whether they heard everything I said or not, I am not sure. But, I hope they were able to understand that I was offended by the way they gave the food. They did that because this was how they felt about the homeless. In their mind, it was ok to just drop food in front of a homeless. Some homeless are indeed mentally ill and they can react violently to folks handing them some food. But, I was out, therefore, selling books as a homeless self-published author and did not exhibit any behavior that will make anyone afraid to hand me some left-over.

If you want to give your left-over to a poor person, be kind enough to ask him or her, hand it to them just like you would like anybody to hand you any gift and not just drop it on the ground. And even then, let them know what you are giving them and give them a chance to accept it or refuse it.

One evening, a group of folks, about four or five of them, walked to me and handed me some left-over. Sometimes I just take the food out of respect for those who hand it to me, but I didn't care about food since I was out there selling my books and making enough money to get me some food, on my way to my tent, after I was finished. "What is it, I asked the man in the group who had his hand stretched towards me with the box of food in his hand". "What does it matter what food it is? Be lucky somebody gives you some food", he interjected while retracting his hand and walked away with the food and his friends. They walked back towards the restaurant entrance and handed the food to a homeless man shining shoes thirty feet away from me. I asked him what was it, as he was opening the box to check the food inside." Some steak" he responded. "I just got some teeth pulled and I can't eat that," I said loudly so that the guys who gave the food could understand why I asked them what food it was to take or kindly refuse it.

When you give to a person in need, something that you have no use for anymore and want to get rid of but don't want to trash away, at least give it with kindness and not with contempt and arrogance. And also, do not feel like a person should take what you offer because he or she is needy and has no choice but be grateful to you for giving him or her whatever you offer them. If you offer a rare or medium-cooked steak to an old homeless person, ask yourself whether they have enough teeth in their mouth to eat it. Never look down on a person because he is less fortunate than you. His or her humanity is equal to yours.

Do not feed anybody in need, food that you would not eat yourself unless you know for sure that they have no problem with it. I use food here as an example, but my whole point is that if you want to help anybody, offer them something that they will not discard, and that, you will not care about even if you were in need. Make sure that whatever you offer as help, will be valued and appreciated and not be thrown away. I will give an example. Many times, I was in McPherson Park between 15th and Vermont Street, both on K Street in Northwest Washington DC, and witnessed homeless folks feeding pigeons with baloney and peanut butter sandwiches handed to them by the food truck coming there to feed the homeless every evening. Many of the Sandwiches were abandoned on the benches or just thrown in the trash bins, by the homeless after the van left. I am very convinced that the folks handing the baloney and peanut butter sandwiches on those vans, would not eat them themselves. The sandwiches seem to have been made and kept in fridges for a long time. You could barely tell the peanut butter from the jelly because the sandwiches were stale.

Unless you know for a fact that the reality that others are going through, do not make assumptions and erroneous judgment, to justify why you refuse to help them.

It was chilly outside. I left my tent with an Eddie Bauer jacket on. The price tag on it said $600 when I was offered it. I was very reluctant to wear it when I was outside selling my book. But it was a very warm and comfortable jacket for the weather in that season. I normally put another jacket on top to hide the Eddy Bauer logo when I sit outside and sell my books. My signs on each side of the low square fence surrounding the tree next to which I sit, say "Help Self-Published Homeless Writer. Get your copy of my book". I was therefore normally expecting some of the folks walking by to feel some kind of way about a person claiming to be homeless but wearing such an expensive piece jacket. A couple approached me. The man, a white male, asked me about the book. He picked a copy and was glancing through it while asking me questions about the book. His female friend and most likely girlfriend or wife, who was an Asian woman, maybe Korean, or Japanese, asked me if I was homeless and if I really wrote the book, and how come I had a cellphone if I was homeless, and then she looked at my Jacket and made a comment about it, then said something to her friend and they dropped the copy immediately and walked away. The jacket was offered to me by a lady who is a lawyer and has her office down the street.

I guess these folks never gave away old clothes to charity. Otherwise, they will not be surprised to see a homeless man wear a Nike shoe or a designer's jacket that was given to him from a clothing room at a church or a closet of a charity.

The most ridiculous thing I ever experienced from folks making an erroneous judgment on others, was when a guy saw me pull my phone from my jacket to respond to a call while I was selling my book on the street. He had a blanket covering my legs while sitting on the low metal fence by a tree on the edge of the sidewalk. He walked from the sidewalk to the tree behind me to look at my phone. "You got a phone; I have seen it. Why are you pretending to be homeless? Shame on you." He screamed at me.

I just could not fathom any commonsensical reason why having a phone would be any evidence that a person is faking homelessness. Do not look for excuses to justify your apathy for the homeless. Stop thinking that all homeless and poor people should look a certain way. There are a lot of people that you see every day who have nowhere to sleep when night comes. They dress nice, smell good, some even have a car, and a job, but are not able to afford rent. When night comes, they sleep in their car or a tent, or at a homeless shelter, or anywhere where they can find a quiet spot. There are a lot of folks around you who look good but cannot feed themselves and their kids. Their fridge stays empty the only food they can afford is what they can purchase with government-issued food stamps.

Do not be malicious and unkind to others, unless you want to infect others with your unhappiness. I have seen folks screaming at beggars: Go get a job" and other unkind words. You never know when you can lose a job. You never know when you get be afflicted by a bad situation which can cause you to lose not just a job, but everything including your health or loved ones. You don't even know if you are going to be alive the next day. So, be grateful for what you have including your life, and be kind to those who are going through a hard time. Help somebody if you can.

One day, a family who went to the restaurant, send their kids outside to tell me that their parents wanted to buy me some food if I needed any. I accepted and they asked me what I wanted and what I wanted on it since they proposed a sandwich and I accepted. They went back in and brought the food back when it was ready. On many other occasions, folks seeing me selling my book outside, sent a waiter or waitress outside to take my order and bring to me, the food that they paid for me when it was ready.

Be kind to others and the universe will send happiness through kindness your way.

Chapter 5

That I have to have a source of income

One lesson that living in hell has taught me is that, I always have to have a means of income to generate enough money to take care of myself. It was a time when I had to go to soup kitchens to feed myself, and it is ok to seek and get help if you don't have enough money and are not making enough to take care of yourself. Trust me, I feel very embarrassed and a little ashamed to even write about it.

I feel like there is nothing more dehumanizing than having to rely on somebody else for food, clothes, and everything else that is needed to survive daily. But at the same time, there is no shame in being humble and getting some help. If you are in that situation, don't feel bad, it is ok. Get all the help you need. If you have to go to a soup kitchen or get handouts so you won't starve, please get the help until you can get a good job and create a means to make money on your own.

Don't let your pride dig your hole deeper and make your life harder, because you are too ashamed to go and get some help or accept help. I have been there done that. When I felt like I had to beg, I did it. That is how I was able to purchase a laptop and write a book and make a lot of money from that book. You got to do what you got to do to take care of yourself. But, the best way to do it, is to either find a job that pays you well enough and that you can live off or come up with some kind of business that you can make enough money off and sustain yourself.

I have worked minimum wage jobs that were not paying enough. But it was better to earn something than nothing. Whatever job that you have now and is helping you even if it is not as much as you desire, just do it until you find better. I did that when I had no other options. But, I came to the point where I didn't want to work to just survive and remain poor for the rest of my life. I want to be rich in my life one day, honest truth. I know what to be poor is like. Now I have to experience what being wealthy is also like before my time comes to exit this life. I appreciate hand-outs and I am so grateful to anybody and everybody who helped me with food, money, and everything else. But, I have to get out of poverty sooner than later.

Until the powers of this world find a replacement to money, or unless you are in a part of the world where you own your land, and can build your own house and grow your food and live off the land, there is no way you and I can live in this world without money. Let's be for real. You need money for everything at this age. The world is under the system of capitalism. Whether we like it or not, the reality is that in such a system, you need money to be able to survive. You need money to have food unless you grow it yourself. You need money to buy, build or rent a house. You need money to get medicine to get well. You even need money to get water to drink unless you own well. Water is abundant in nature but human beings find a way to sell it to one another. This is crazy. But that is the reality we are living in. Hopefully, we will not have to buy the air we breathe every day.

Without money, you will just be poor and hungry and homeless and needy mostly if you are in a developed nation, but also a developing and underdeveloped nation as well.

I was selling my book on the street one day and a person who bought my copy told me that she was making a hundred thousand a year as income but she still was not happy with her life. I looked at her and told myself, "Somebody please, give me a hundred thousand dollars each year, I will be very happy with my life".

No matter how you feel about money, it is what it is. You need it and you need to make a lot of it to be able to live a sustainable life. Is money or the love of it, the root of all evil? I don't necessarily or completely agree. There was a time when human societies did not use money for anything. Yet, evil existed. Evil is in the negative motives such as greed, selfishness, wickedness that makes folks harm others to have more of anything including money. Other than that, some people have plenty of money and do help others with it. So, you need money, a lot of money. Now, what you do with it, or how you behave because you have plenty of it, is your issue.

You have to either work or create a reliable source of income for yourself to earn what you need to be self-reliant.

There is a right and a wrong way to make money. Resist the temptation to make money the wrong way. You will get caught and go to jail and lose everything. It does not matter if you are a poor man stealing to make money, or a rich man embezzling thousands or millions of dollars, it is not worth it. Don't listen to that voice that tells you to try to make money any other way than working for it or creating your source of income the right way.

You may not like your job, but be grateful you have a job and make sure you find another job before quitting the one that is putting money in your pocket now. Unemployment may not last forever. If you are tired of working for other people and taking orders, create your source of income. Be an entrepreneur, but make sure you know what you are doing and that you can run a business and provide the service that your business is about.

You cannot be forever dependent on public assistant or charity unless you are incapacitated or disabled. If you need public assistance or charity because you cannot find employment or cannot work for whatever reason, then do not feel bad to seek and accept assistance.

Even if you have to beg, do not feel bad about doing it as long as you do not make it a way of life but only something of last resort out of extreme desperation. Sometimes in life, you have to put your pride on the side and do what you got to do to survive until things get better. I did it, I mean I went on the street and beg for money and I am not ashamed of it. This was the most humbling thing I had to do. I did it so I could get enough money to buy a laptop and use it to write a book. Thank God I did. Today I can sell thousands of copies of the book I wrote with the laptop I bought with the money I made by panhandling on the same street that I came back to sell my book on. Today, I don't have to ever go back on the street and beg again. I am still begging through Paypal and Venmo like everybody else. It is very ironic that society shame poor people who resort to begging to earn money, but a system has been created through technology and social media to make people beg online through platforms like Gofundme, Cashap, Paypal, and tons of other sites that make money off you begging though them. So, a person who solicits money for donation through a charity or a money app is not doing anything different than a poor man or woman shaking a cup on the street corner. They are all asking for money. The only problem is that the poor man or woman is called a beggar, but the one with cash up is not.

I got Venmo and Paypal and from time to time, I ask people to send me donations through either medium. It is just a more dignifying way of begging than shaking a cup on the street corner, but it is all the same. To believe that it is different is just an illusion. By the way, you are welcome to send me any donation anytime at Paypal.me/leognawa or venmo@leognawa. I am a self-publish activist writer and I survive by selling my books. That is my job. I got to sell books every day to be able to survive. Now that I have my own place and am no longer homeless, I have to sell my books every day to be able to pay my rent. My rent is $1500 a month, utilities included. That means that I have to sell at least 200 copies of my books per month. A little over half the money I make from every copy I sell goes towards purchasing my copies at the author's price and covering the cost of packaging and shipping.

As an activist and author, I can use donations to make up for the time I am not selling books.

So far, I can sell enough copies of my book to keep a roof over my head, fill my fridge with all the food I desire, and also give to the homeless man and woman shaking a cup in my face without worrying about what they are going to do with the money. That is their business. Once I gave money to a man or woman who is in a situation that I have through and that I perfectly understand, I am not worried whether they go purchase some alcohol or drug with it. All I know is that I did my part to help them as others help me. If they misuse that money, they are the ones who will suffer the consequence.

Do whatever you need to do to make some money as long as you are not doing anything against the law and not doing harm and not scamming or taking advantage of or anybody.

If you have to drive Uber or Lyft, go ahead do it. If you have to start a Youtube channel, give it a try. It is a lot of YouTubers who make a lot of money by just talking and having people listen to them. There few youtube channels that I follow myself, mostly those of folks documenting their travels. I noticed that as soon as they come online for a live, many of the viewers just send donations in to support them.

It is obvious to me that if you produce or do something that people like, they will support you. I myself was a little reluctant to ask for donations on my social media platform, but when I watch youtube and see folks donating to their favorite channels, it makes me feel less ashamed to ask for donations on the social media that I post on daily to inspire and motivate my readers.

I chose to be an entrepreneur as my means of generating an income. So, I have to be well organized for my endeavors to be fruitful. It is a lot of hard work. It is not easy.

Today in 2021, reality is not what it was before the Coronavirus Pandemic. And even before the Corona Pandemic, corporations in their greed for more and more profit had created more machines and used more electronics to replace human labor. Decades ago, there were more cashiers

81

in stores. Today, there are more self-service machines that replaced cashiers at most grocery stores. In years to come, they might be self-driving cars that will not need drivers. There will therefore be fewer drivers needed, fewer cashiers needed, fewer workers needed in a near future. There will be fewer and fewer jobs available in a not-so-distant future. You might end up becoming homeless if you don't have a job or a source of income.

It will come a time when governments will no longer print money and give it to you as a stimulus. You are going to have to figure out how to earn money. Walk around the downtown of your city if you live in America or Canada and maybe in developed nations of Europe and you will see more homeless on the streets. Anytime I ride my bike in downtown Washington DC these days, I see tents spreading everywhere like grass. Every Park in the city is now a homeless tent city except a very few. Tents are everywhere on sidewalks.   The number of homeless is growing in Washington DC from what I see every day.

It is time for you to be the best at everything you do because only the best will survive better than the rest.

There was a time when I used to do a lot of day jobs. I was staying at a shelter at CCNV, on Second and D Street Norwest Washington DC. Contractors looking for laborers came there to pick up homeless men and women waiting to go work. I started working daily with a guy about my age, who picked me up once and made me a regular of his laborers since. Whenever these folks looking for workers pulled up in front or at the corner of the shelter, they had to pick a few among the crowd of homeless men and women waiting since the early in the morning to be picked to go to work. The idea that people are homeless because they do not want to work is crazy. There are more homeless folks going to work every day than the one you see on the street begging.

Anyway, the guy was called Mike, I think. He was very friendly and so many homeless guys wanted to work for him, but he could only get but a few, about 4 or 5. Once, I started working with him, he put me in charge when he dropped us on the job and had to leave us there to go handle some business somewhere else. Riding with him was something else. He had a pick-up truck and always had me with him, in the front, with another worker while the rest were riding with the tools and trash cans, in the back of the pick-up truck. He used to smoke weed throughout the trip. He also used to pay me more than the other workers who were getting forty dollars for the eight hours he had us working for him. He was giving me sixty dollars instead and did not want me to let the others know that he was giving me more money than them. One day, he took us to Georgetown, an upscale neighborhood in the western part of Washington, DC. He had a contract there with a Jewish synagogue to dig a pool there. Jews have a form of baptism like Christian and use the pool for that practice. I can't remember how long we took to complete the job, but maybe a week, I guess. It was about four of us plus Mike. He used to just drop us there and put me in charge. We had a jackhammer, a wheelbarrow, some buckets, and few more tools. I used to stay on the jackhammer most of the time because I wanted to make sure the most important part of the job was done. Many times, some of the other guys, most of them in their twenties were getting mad at me because I kept working when they were taking long breaks. By keeping digging with the jackhammer, I was accumulating more dirt that they had to pick up. I was therefore creating more work for them in case Mike showed up and saw me working and the rest resting while the dirt and rocks and gravels were piling up in the hole I was digging.

If you work for anybody, make sure they are happy about your work. And make sure you are enjoying what you are doing.

It is ok to do a job that you may not like but is paying your bills, is keeping a roof over your head, and is putting food on your table until you can find something else that is better. Apply yourself and do your job with devotion so that whoever you work for or whoever is a boss over you, can find you indispensable.

If you feel like you can no longer tolerate whatever makes you unhappy at your job, and be smart and wise about how you are going to handle the situation.

Do not just quit a job and get yourself fired and find yourself without any means to survive. Look for another one while still keeping the one you got until you find something better.

No matter how much confidence you have in yourself or faith you have in divine providence or good luck, do not let emotions make you make a decision that will be detrimental to you and jeopardize your sole means of income.

You cannot simply expect money to fall from the sky no matter how much confident you are that your wishes will come true or how long to spend on your knees praying for miracles or how many lottery tickets you play.

You have to put work in and try hard to find a job. Situations may arise that might make it hard for you to find employment. If you are not able to find suitable employment that will generate the ideal income for you, seek other means of generating income. There is always something you can do for yourself as an entrepreneur. I am not telling you to start your own business unless it is something you think you are capable of doing. Because I was told by few folks who read the articles that I wrote in 2005 in the Street Sense Homeless newspaper that I was a good writer, I thought I could make a living from writing books.

But I was uncertain whether I should write a book about my homeless experience at first when someone suggested that I do so. My emotions got in the way at first. I was ashamed of being homeless and I was not very proud of writing a book and tell the whole world that I was homeless. But I told myself that, I could not hide forever the fact that I was homeless; that I could make a lot of money selling my book; I could find my purpose as an activist, creating awareness about homelessness as an activist.

Those three reasons were convincing enough to cast my emotions aside and do what was necessary to create an opportunity to create my own business through entrepreneurship. I went ahead a wrote the book. I titled it Homeless Lives Matter, Homeless My story. I wrote the book under harsh conditions. Because I was staying in a tent, I had to find somewhere

84

indoors where I could write peacefully. It was a very cold winter. In the day, I went to Northwest One Neighborhood Library located at 55 L St NW. At night I went to the FedEx store on 16th and K street, in Norwest Washington C. The store was open twenty-four hours a day. I would stay and write there from around 11 pm until or 5 am, then catch the first 80 bus around 5:30 am to North Capitol and Michigan avenue NE, then walk about 10 minutes to my tent up on North Capitol Street. But sometimes, when I was in my tent at night and felt inspired, I would wake up and turn my laptop on and write in the cold. My fingers were frozen at times. I used to put them between my thighs to warm them with my body heat and then kept writing until they were too frozen, then I stopped and went to sleep until my pile of four or five blankets and covers until the morning. To even get a laptop to start with, I decided to go and beg on the street for money. It took me a lot of humility to bring myself to beg on the street. I will discuss humility in another chapter.

I went to purchase the laptop at Micro Center on Nutley Street, in Fairfax, Virginia after I raised enough money from begging on the street. I waited until after the Christmas and the New Year holidays to get the laptop during the Holiday sale. I got something very cheap on sale. It cost me about 300 dollars.

It took me about 4 months to finish the book. I don't remember what happened, but I damaged the laptop. Did I leave it in the tent and it got rained on when I left the tent uncovered? Most likely. I took it to the same computer store where I bought it so it could be fixed. I had a one-year guarantee on it which to me meant that the repair was at no cost. A week or so later, I received a call from Micro Center. The lady on the phone told me that they could turn the computer back on and that I could come and pick it up. I was happy. But, before I head to the store, she called me back and told me that an electrical incident happened while she was working on the hard drive. She told me that my data needed to be moved to another hard drive but the store did not have the proper equipment for that particular laptop brand, which was an Acer. She told me, I had to pay something like $500 for the laptop to be sent to another store for the problem to be fixed. I told her, no way. I had a guarantee that did not expire. Besides, the new problem was not my fault but the result of an incident caused by the technician working on the computer. So how could they charge me to fix the problem caused by one of their technicians? Then they call me back and told me that the warranty did not cover data transfer, therefore if I wanted the damaged hard drive repaired, it would cost me five hundred dollars, or they could replace the hard drive by ordering a new one from the manufacturer. The only problem was that they would not transfer the data from the old hard drive to the new one unless I paid for it. I told them to go ahead and order a new one. They called me a couple of weeks later to come and pick my laptop with the new hard drive installed on it. My idea was that I was going to ask them to give me the old hard drive so I could get somebody else to get the data out of it and get in on my new hard drive. But when I got there and ask them for the old hard drive, I was told that the hard drive was returned to the manufacturer in exchange for the replaced hard drive.

Everything I wrote for 5 months prior, was on the hard drive they damaged. I never saved anywhere else, anything I wrote all that time. I had finished the book and was about to edit it and print it. Now, everything was lost. I was so devastated. I had no idea what to do.

Imagine yourself in that situation. How would have you felt? If you ever find yourself in such a situation. can be any situation in life. You may have put a lot of time and energy into accomplishing something, but an accident or incident or situation happened that caused you to lose everything that you have accomplished. I know how devastating it is and depressing it can get. I have been there, so I understand. When all the work you did for months or years, is lost, do not give up, start over again. I know it is not easy to overcome the depression that results from having to start over a project that is lost. But I did it.

I wrote the book over from memory. But it was not that hard because it seems like I had memorized every sentence of it. It took me no time to rewrite the book. Once I finished it, I got it printed and sold it on the street. It was not easy at all, but it was rewarding. I sold two books per hour on average. The longer I stayed out, the more money I made. Sometimes, it was extremely slow and I did not sell any book for a couple of hours although hundreds of pedestrians passing by me. But, when I was about to give up and pack up and live because I was getting too frustrated with nobody buying my book, all of a sudden, one person after another will show up back-to-back and purchase copies. I would then get three or four sales in the next hour. Though I was selling my book for ten dollars a copy, about twenty to 30 percent of my customers offered me a twenty-dollar bill and asked me to keep the change. Many folks also gave me money for the book but asked me to give the book to someone else, since they were on their way to a club or to a bar and did not want to carry the book with them.

When the Corona Virus hit, I was no longer able to sell my book on the streets because the Mayor had ordered a total shutdown of the city. Everybody was ordered to stay indoors and not come out but only to shop for groceries or take care of urgent needs.

Though I was making enough money to take care of basic needs, I was not saving enough to get a place yet. You have to save some of your income, otherwise, you will be working hard and not have any money left after you pay your bills and take care of basic needs. You will end up paying rent in the same place for years, but once you lose your job or find yourself in a situation when you can no longer pay your rent, you will be evicted from the place you paid rent every month for years.

If possible, try to save ten percent of every check you receive from your job. Imagine how much money you will save in a year, in two years, in five years. I know it is easier said than done, but it is not impossible to do. If you do that, you will have enough money to fall back on when hard times hits.

It is good to be generous, but do not give more than you can afford to. This has been my issue. I have given a lot of money to others in need. I have given way too much, the reason why I never saved enough to get myself a place to live despite making enough every day from selling my book.

When the Corona Virus hit, I was no longer able to sell copies of my book on the street. I had enough money to survive for a while since I did not have to worry about paying rent because I was living in my tent. But it was getting chilly because the weather was transitioning into the winter. I didn't want to deal with cold weather this time, at the end of the year 2020 and the start of 2021. I decided to spend more nights on a friend's couch. I offered him twenty dollars per night whenever I decided to go to his apartment when it was cold outside and I didn't feel like sleeping in my tent.

I had to figure a new way to sell my book. I remember a couple of black ladies who had stopped in front of my book one day and implored me to advertise my book on the social media platform called Instagram. I did not know much about Instagram and was not interested in their plea. I was telling myself silently, "you guys are not buying my book, but you are wasting my time telling me about social media, I wish you could keep moving". I remembered the two ladies when I was in my tent trying to figure out how to sell my books online and attract as many customers a day as I used to when selling my books on 15th Street. Whatever you do in life that is working for or is beneficial to you, don't give up or stop because situations have changed and you are no longer able to do it as you used to. Just find a new way and readjust to the new reality. I knew with the Coronavirus, more people will stay home, and will purchase online and read more because they were nothing much to do with everything shut and closed. So, this was a new opportunity for me to reach new customers online instead of crying about not be able to have customers on the streets as I used to.

Even in the worse of situations, there are always opportunities because there is an increase in needs that be serviced through entrepreneurship. Do not jump off the bridge because reality has changed. Find new ways to doing things and adapt. To the new reality.

I had to set up a website as soon as possible and sell my books on it. The book was on Amazon but, I had to wait every sixty days to received royalty payments for copies sold on Amazon. I had someone helping me setting up a webpage linked to an e-commerce site and an online payment platform account linked to a bank account. Then I created an Instagram account using the same name Homelesslivesmatterbook as my website name. I had a little over seven thousand followers a year later. I sold about two thousand books online within a year. In February 2021, I was to find a place to rent. I used a little half of the money I made, to pay for my copies from the manufacturer, order and pay for packing and shipping supplies and cost, and also pay few people who help me packing and taking packages to the post office. I also donated a lot of some of my profit to other people in need.

When you are going through hard life and an opportunity to make money shows up, do not misuse and waste that money. Use it for your most urgent needs and then save some of it and then use the rest for whatever. But do not worry about fun and having fun and buying expensive clothes and partying until you have a roof over your head or have enough to keep a roof over your head.

When I used to walk to my tent and was getting very tired, I use to push myself by chanting the following words "the faster I walk, the closer I get, the faster I walk, the closer I get, the faster I walk, the closer I get" and kept moving until I reached my tent.

 One thing I can admit is that I am lazy by nature. I like to relax and take too long to do things even though I know they are urgent. And I end up being pressed for time and having too much to do in a short time when I realize that I have wasted too much time.

I will give you a perfect example. Last year around my birthday, I had a hundred copies of my book Homeless Lives Matter, Homeless My story stored at a friend's house. I decided to do fundraising by asking folks on social media to order my book from November 20 to November 26, so I could make $1500 by my birthday which was on November 27. On the first day, I received only one order. But on November 22 and mostly on November 23, to my surprise, I receive about 1000 orders on both days. I was shocked. That was at least $15,000 made in two days. Though about half of that money was my profit, it was still enough money for me to be looking for a place to live and no longer be homeless. I also received some donations, which made the total reach a little over 20,000 dollars. What a birthday present that was? But here was the problem. I only had 100 books. That means that I had to order a little over a thousand copies of my book from the manufacturer and then wait until then to get to my friend's apartment before I ship them to those who ordered them. When I got a little over thousand orders by November 23, my dumb ass stopped the fundraiser by telling people that I had reached my goal and that there was no longer any need to keep ordering.

But anyway, I was grateful for such an unexpected blessing. I always planned to start looking for a place to live when I have enough money saved to afford at least 6 months of rent. So, I estimated that half of the $20,000 will be my profit and could be used towards renting an apartment and furnish it.

I needed more books, so I ordered 2000 books. It cost me about 7000 dollars. I had to wait for about 10 days to 2 weeks for the books to be delivered.

But here is the problem. I just took a break instead of using the time that I was waiting to get all the envelopes I needed and prepare them in advance. I had enough time, to order 2000 envelopes and print all the names and addresses of the orders and stick them on the envelopes while waiting for the books to come. I did not do that. I waited until the book came about ten days later, to start trying to find the right envelopes. Instead of ordering everything online one time, I ask someone to get me envelopes at some Staples and Home Depot stores in Virginia. Some of the envelopes were padded, others were just regular paper envelopes.

90

When the books came, I realize that I a lot of work to do. The first thing I needed to do, was to download the format of the address labels I was going to use and then go to a FedEx store and print them, then stick them on the packages, then go to ship them.

I took my time doing all that and realize that it was taking forever. More orders came in and I had about 1400 orders by January 2021. I only shipped a quarter of those orders and still had three quarters to be shipped. Throughout December I processed the orders and took almost 50 packages to the post office daily. I worked all night and all day and only rested for 3 or 4 hours. First I had to open every box containing about 40 books, Then I put each book in a Ziploc bag to protect them from any covid 19 contamination from the time they live my hand to the time they get to whoever ordered them. Then I had to insert every book into an envelope. Then I had to go online and copy and paste every shipping address of every order on the template that I downloaded on my laptop until I completed about 5 or 6 pages. The address label template had 10 spaces. Then I had to go to FedEx and print the labels, about 50 at a time. Then I had to come back to my friend's apartment and stick the labels on the envelopes. Then I had to stick the return address labels on each envelope also. Then, I had to take the packages to the post office and ship them.

It was a lot of work, but it became harder work because I did not do it right. Work smart, don't work hard is an idiom I did not apply. One big mistake I made was to use stamps to speed the process. It was during the holiday season (Thanksgiving Christmas and New Year's Day), The line was longer at the post office. I took about 25 packages to the counter at the post office on North Capitol and Massachusetts Avenue sometimes in the morning and had a friend take 25 more in the evening and vice versa. I was paying him to do that. Soon, the clerks at the post office starting whining that I was having too many packages. They suggested other means but when I checked on the United Postal Service (USPS) website, media mail, which I used, did not qualify (I got to check on the USPS site to properly quote them).

One of the clerks suggested that I use stamps. I went ahead a purchase 1000 stamps of $2.80 each. That was another $2800 less of the profit I made. To make a story short, it took me until the end of January to ship all the books. But, a lot of folks starting complaining to me that they did not receive their copies. The return address that I was using was someone else. The person never told me that dozens of packages were returned to their address. I found that later that many of the packages were returned, lost, or damage because of the poor quality of the envelope for the most part, but also because of poor handling of the packages by the post office.

Some of the folks who ordered my book sent me a picture of the empty envelopes they received with no book inside. It was a mess. Although most of the 1200 folks who ordered their copy during that November fundraiser received their copies, a few hundred did not.

I had to resend a little over hundred copies that were either sent back or lost. This was a huge cut on my profit, but I did ok in the end.

The lesson I learned here is that I should have planned this thing much better and in a better-disciplined manner. It would have saved me time and money.

What I did for future orders to prevent the same situation from happening was that, I went online and find a cheap padded envelope manufacturer and order in bulk for very cheap. The second thing I did was packaging the book in envelopes in advance and getting address label printing right after I had enough orders. So, I did a few things to make it easier and faster to deliver on my orders.

One of the problems I had was that it took me too long to execute the great ideas I always had. I am always postponing things and always end up doing things later than sooner. Please do what you got to do sooner than later. You will come up better. If you wait too long to get things done, you may miss out on opportunities that may never come back around. There are things in your life that you need to do now, or it will be too late later.

Chapter 6

That I have to think and act wisely

One of the lessons that living a hard life taught me, is to always think, decide and act wisely.

Always remind yourself to make wise decisions. Wisdom will make life easier and better for you.   I survived through rough times by taking the time to think very seriously and deeply before I made any move or did anything major many a time, not all the time, but most of the time, and it paid off pretty well.

What is wisdom? I checked in the two topmost renowned dictionaries of the English language and this is what they say. According to the England-based oxford dictionary, wisdom is the ability to make sensible decisions and give good advice because of the experience and knowledge that you have. And also, as the knowledge that a society or culture has gained over a long time. The Merriam Webster, America's most popular dictionary has wisdom defined as the ability to discern inner qualities and relationships. And also, as good sense, generally accepted belief, accumulated philosophical or scientific learning.

Wisdom to me is the ability to think, decide and act intelligently, and control emotions, to prevent a detrimental and negative reaction and consequence and achieve a positive and desirable outcome in solving problems and dealing with situations, other humans, and reality.

In other words, you have to always think of the consequence and reactions to the way you think, decide and act by being able to predict whether they are going to be negative or positive.

Be smart

So many times, I have done things or reacted in a certain way and regretted it later. Think about how many times have you done things or reacted a certain way and told yourself later " I wished I never done that"? It happens to all of us every day.

Most of the time, we do not think, act, or react wisely because we get too emotional, too angry, too impulsive, too desperate, too excited, too gullible, too unreasonable or too impatient.

Road rage is a perfect case in point. It is so crazy to see drivers screaming, insulting, and threatening one another because one person thought that the one in front of them was driving too slowly. There have been instances when folks came out of their cars to fight one another over nothing that serious. Some drivers went as far as pulling a gun and shooting bullets into the other car. Last month on May 21, 2021, Aiden Leos, a 6-year-old boy sitting in the passenger side in his mother's car, turned towards him and told her that his stomach was hurting. When she turned towards him to check on him, her boy was drenched in blood and died by the time an ambulance showed up.

Yesterday, June 8, 2021, Marcus Anthony Eriz, 24, has been charged with felony murder and discharge of a gun at an inhabited dwelling, with sentencing enhancements for causing death. His girlfriend, Wynne Lee, 23, was charged with accessory after the fact and concealing a firearm in the vehicle.

Marcus shot the car from behind because the mother of the 6-year-old showed him a finger when she had cut in front of the car his girlfriend was driving. The bullet when through the trunk and ended in the boy's stomach.

They were arrested and charged yesterday. They are in jail awaiting trial. I am quite sure they both feel very stupid now. This is what people when they lack wisdom and are not able to control their emotions at the moment. I am quite sure if shot in the tank thinking that he was only going to scare the woman. He probably had no idea that the bullet would have traveled from the trunk to the front sit and lodge into a 6-year-old boy's stomach. Now you kill a child because you wanted to show how bad you are. Now you have taken the life of an innocent little boy who was in kindergarten.

I want to share an excerpt of a Washington Post article of March 2016 about a teenager who killed another teenager for staring at him.

The article is titled, D.C. police arrest suspect in the fatal shooting of 15-year-old at Deanwood Metro

by Peter Hermann and Keith L. Alexander March 29, 2016

The 15-year-old was sitting on a bench with his mother and younger sisters inside a glass shelter, waiting for a train at the Deanwood Metro station in Northeast. Davonte Washington, his head bowed, was absorbed in his cellphone.

An older teenager clutching a white bag with carryout food walked by on the platform with friends. One of Davonte's sisters looked at the young man after he had passed. He paused and tapped on the glass to draw Davonte's attention.

Davonte stepped out.

They exchanged words. "What the f--- you keep looking at me for? You know me from somewhere?" the older teen uttered, police said. A split second later, without provocation or for no more reason than what the gunman may have taken as a disrespectful glance, "the suspect pulled a silver or chrome handgun and shot" Davonte, police said.

95

The police arrest affidavit says the gunman handed his food to a friend, tucked his gun in his pants, and fled the station, with Davonte's mother racing after him shouting: "Stop him! He just shot my son!"

Teen arrested in death of 15-year-old at Deanwood Metro

D.C. Police have charged Maurice Bellamy, 17, with second-degree murder while armed in the death of 15-year-old Davonte Washington, who was fatally shot on the platform of the Deanwood Metro station the day before Easter. (WUSA9)

Police outlined a chilling scenario Tuesday in a court document as well as in a courtroom, charging Maurice Bellamy, 17, of Southeast Washington as an adult with second-degree murder while armed in Saturday afternoon's slaying. Davonte was gunned down in front of his mother and sisters at 4 p.m. as he was headed to get a haircut for Easter, his family said.

Police said they have no evidence that the suspect and Davonte knew each other.

[Teen fatally shot on Metro platform in front of mother, sisters]

The lack of motive confounded D.C. Police Chief Cathy L. Lanier, long accustomed to explaining deadly violence stemming from petty disputes yet struggling to explain the District's 26th killing of 2016.

"When it comes to violence, nothing is more senseless than this case, in my opinion," the chief said. "The loss of a 15-year-old boy under any circumstances is a tragedy. But in this case, it's even more so, as it appears that there was just no reason for it. No reason for it.",

(Source: https://www.washingtonpost.com/local/public-safety/dc-police-arrest-suspect-in-fatal-shooting-of-15-year-old-at-deanwood-metro/2016/03/29/38181710-f510-11e5-8b23-538270a1ca31_story.html).

So you, young man, killed another young man in front of his mother and little sisters simply because the young man looked at you. Did you know that the young man did not live with his mother and that that day was one of the few occasions he had to spend some time with his mother and young sisters? Did you know that he was on his way to get a haircut? What kind of heart or mind shall I say do have to do some stupid and evil like this? Now, you have ended another young man's life and messed up your life for good.

I am sure you are sitting in prison and regretting what you did. You are probably telling yourself that pulling a gun and killing someone because they stared at you, was not a wise thing to do.

 I spent a lot of time on the streets as a homeless person for a long time. I have seen kids acting very unkindly, unruly, and disrespectfully even towards folks old enough to be their grandparents. The first thing I used to tell myself, was" Who is raising these kids? Why are their parents allowing them to behave like that"?

One day, I got on the bus number 80 on 12th and H street. It was about 9 pm. I had just finished selling my book and was heading to my tent. The bus usually takes about 15 minutes to get there. I get there on my bike in about 30 minutes. I went to sit in the back of the bus by the window on the right side. There were about 4 other passengers on the bus. The bus arrived at Gallery Place Chinatown two stops later. Few more passengers got on it. One of them was a young man who walked all the way to the back and sat by the windows on the left side. He looked like he was probably in his late teens or early twenties. Another young man screaming from outside of the bus sprinted inside to the back and physically held the other young man in the neck and threatened to kill him. Other passengers sitting around moved to the front of the bus probably out of fear. I stood there with the desire to get involved but I was just observing because the young man threatening the other young man, did not strike or hit him. He just had his hand on his neck and was uttering threats like " I will kill you if you do this again". The bus driver never moved the bus and never intervened until the other guy walked away and out of the bus and back to the bus stop.

The driver then closed the bus and started moving out of the bus stop. I checked on the young man at the back of the bus on the left side of me to make sure he was ok. Then, I told the bus driver that he should call for help and report the incident. A lady in a wheelchair who was sitting in the front of the bus, yelled back at me" Mind your business, he did not hurt him, so there is no need for the bus driver to do anything". Then when I responded that I disagreed with her, she opened the window and shouted something at the young man who was still at the bus stop while the bus was halfway to the next stop on 8th Street. The young man raced from 7th street to the stop on 8th street. Traffic was slow, so the bus was not moving fast. He got in the doorway when the driver opened the door and threatened to kill me while staying by the bus driver and threatening me. I raced from the back of the bus and jump on him and pushed him on the bus driver's wheel and held on his hand. He had a pouch in his hand and I assumed he had a gun in there because he was so confident about killing people. I did not want to give him any chance to pull anything out of that bag whether it was a gun or just a knife in it. I had his head against the bus driver's wheel and all my body wait on him. He was a shorter dude and I was physically stronger than him. While I had him pinned down on the bus driver's wheel, I insisted that the bus driver call the police. The young guy kept screaming " Get off me, get off me". I said to him that I was not going to get off him until the police showed up. The young man, scream out for help from his friends who were at the other station. Three of them raced to the bus, and got behind me, and start pulling me off him. One held my neck in a chokehold. I had to free my hand to try to remove my head from the chokehold, but I managed to snatch the ouch from the young man who ran outside of the bus. The other two of his friend got the pouch off my hand while I struggled to free myself from the man holding my neck. All of them made it out of the bus and run towards 7th street. I started chastising the bus driver and blame him for the entire incident. The police showed up about a minute later. They took a statement from me, the driver, and the young man who I stood for and who was in the back of the bus. Then they had few officers go to the other station and try to find the other young man. About five minutes later they came and threatened to arrest me if I wanted the other young man arrested. I did not understand their reason. They explained to me that when they went to arrest the other man, three of his friend claimed that they witnessed the whole incident and it was me who assaulted their friend and they came to rescue him from me. The police, therefore, asked both me and the young man to forget the whole incident and move on or both were getting arrested. I told the officers, that all they had to do was to view all the cameras on the bus and see who was telling the truth. But, there did not want to hear me. So, I had to do what they asked me to, and they left. The bus driver waited for his boss to show up and write an incident report before the bus continued and dropped me at my destination.

I could have kept arguing with the officers and end up getting unjustly arrested although all I did was preempt a self-defense move on someone threatening to kill me. But I thought the wise thing to do was to let the officers have their way so I could go sleep in my bed in my tent instead of a holding ail cell for the night.

Incidents like that are a common occurrence when you live on the street and are around folks who have no idea of what the meaning of their life is and live a life without purpose.

 I had been homeless off and on for a long time. I have lived in a tent for the last 7 years, and before that, I stay with friends in their apartment and was paying them few bucks a day. The last time I stayed with someone before moving out, was an old homeless man who was an alcoholic. I will not give names here or identify locations. One day, I was sitting on a bench and needed a shower very badly. Another homeless acquaintance of mine walked by and stopped to chat with me. I told him that I needed a shower. He told me that he had a place where he could take me to take one. He showed me a key. I asked whose place that was. He told me that it was his friend's but the friend was not staying there, at the moment. We got on the bus and went to the place. I took a shower and gave the guy who took me there, ten dollars. He told me that I could give him five more dollars to stay there for the day if I wanted. I told him that I was alright, I did not need to stay there. All I needed was a shower. He told me that I could stay if I pay him ten dollars every day. I responded that I would consider doing that only if I meet the owner of the place and get his consent. A few days later, I saw him and another old homeless man. He introduced him to me, and the old man told me that it was ok, for me to stay at his apartment for ten dollars a day. I told him that I will think about it and let him know. We set up a date to meet. I went there a Saturday morning. He was home alone. He begged to stay there. I said ok. I gave him ten dollars and he let me stay in the den. Nobody was sleeping in the bedroom. He was sleeping in the living room. But, as soon as he gave me the key and got the ten dollars, he left. He was panhandling and getting drunk downtown and never came to the apartment for almost a month. I met him downtown by the McDonald on 13th and New York Avenue to give him his money. Sometimes, I did not see him for three or four days, but I kept his money and gave him everything I owed him whenever I saw him. I also rarely saw the friend who initially took me there. One night, I was riding my bike downtown and rode through a small park on Rhode Island and 10th street. I saw an old person on the ground sleeping in the dirt. One shoe was laying on one side and the other, elsewhere. He only had his sucks on. I rode close to him to check on him. It was the old man. I woke him up and told him that I would put" him in a take and take him home. He looked at me while still laying on the ground looking so drunk. "Leo, are you ok in the apartment?" he asked. "Yes, I am, I responded, but you need to go home. It is not safe for you to be laying here asleep" I said back to him. "Leo, don't worry about me, I am not gonna sleep here. I will go and sleep around the church down the street. I do this all the time. I am ok. That is what I want to do. As long as you are ok in the house, I am happy. Don't worry about giving me the money now. Bring it to me tomorrow at McDonald's". I stay in that apartment in North East Washington DC for about three good months by myself. But when the weather started getting cold, he and the guy who introduced me to him started coming to the apartment every night. They spend the time in the living room, one on the couch and the other in the loveseat. Later, the other guy brought his girlfriend in. Three of them stayed in the living room. I stayed in the den but moved to the bedroom. I moved out later to somewhere else for a year but still had my belonging there. Any time I run through the old man, he would ask me when I was coming back home. I finally did come back a year later. . When I moved back there, the son was not staying there but had his belongings there. I moved back to the main bedroom. His son came back but the other couple had moved to the den and the son and his father were in the living room while I was alone in the bedroom. Nobody else was paying the old man but me. Every morning, I will give him ten dollars. He used that money to drink every day and barely ate some food. Sometimes I was making sure he had a meal. I used to go to the carry-out ad get him some friend wings and French fries in addition to the ten dollars. One day, he got very sick and got hospitalized for about two weeks. He had an issue with his liver and got operated on. His son had a girlfriend who was staying there from time to time. Sometimes, for a couple of days, sometimes for a couple of weeks. The son and his girlfriend were sleeping in the living room with the father. The father was sleeping on the couch and the son's girlfriend and the son were sleeping on a mattress on the floor. Sometimes, all of them were drunk and the son and his girlfriend used to get into some violent altercation, then makeup as if nothing happened. While the father was in the hospital, his son left for the store while his girlfriend was in the living room. I was in my bedroom alone listening to some music and trying to sleep. The son came back and started arguing with his girlfriend. Both were drunk. He called my name out loud, then headed to my bedroom. There was a curtain in front of it. I grabbed a butcher knife that I kept under the mattress and stuck it in my pants in my back and cover it with my Tee-shirt. "Leo, why is she naked? "He asked me. "Why are you asking me? I don't know if she is naked or not. I have not been over there and she has not been here," I responded. Then he pulled out a knife and kept asking me whether I did anything with his girl. I pulled my knife out and told him to calm down. I assured him that I would never disrespect his father by doing anything like that. I told him that I appreciated his father letting me staying there and I would not try anything on the girlfriend of his father's son because that will be disrespecting his father in my opinion. He took the knife back to the kitchen. My bedroom was not the kitchen. I turn around with the knife in my hand and walked back towards my room with my back turn away from him. The next thing I know, he snatches the knife out of my hand and acted as if he was going to attack me with it. I jumped on him and grabbed the blade of the knife while wrestling him to the ground. He was a stocky dude but shorter than me. While he fell to the ground, I manage to get on top of him and pulled the knife from his hand while I was holding the blade. I held the knife on top of him. I could have stabbed him without thinking and ruin my entire life with a murder.

J told him to calm down. I got off him and went to wash my bleeding hand. The cut in the palm of my hand was not deep. I went back to my room. I was disturbed and was thinking of moving from out of there for good. He came later and told me that I should leave and I could not stay there anymore. I told him that only his father could tell me to leave and that I will go visit his father in the hospital in the morning but before that. I was not going anywhere. He called the police. When They came, I explained what happened and told them that I was paying his father money to stay there and that I stayed there for a couple of years and he just moved there. I told them that I had brought some of the furniture including the one he was sleeping in. I had got some second-hand furniture at a thrift store and brought them there; a bed and a couch. I left the couch in the living room and had the bed in my bedroom. The police talked to him and came back to talk to me while they had me outside in front of the door. The police told me to just leave for a couple of hours to just de-escalate the situation and by the time I return, he would have calmed down. They assured me that he would not enter my bedroom and touch anything inside. I left, came back, and went to sleep after staying up for a couple more hours, just to make sure that he would not try to provoke or attack me. IN the morning, I showered and went to the hospital to visit his father and explained what happened. His father was already aware because the son called him and explained his version of what happened. The father assured me that nothing like that would ever happen again and that I should not move out. I stayed there until I found out that the son convinced his father to move out to another apartment. I was informed only at the last moment. A couple of days, later, they had moved out to an unknown apartment. None of us staying there, I and the couple knew where they moved to. The guy staying there brought another couple there. Then tried to bring another of his bring. So, I moved out. I went and found a location in a wooded area up on North Capitol Street and later added a tent. I explained all that in detail in the book, Homeless Lives Matter, Homeless My story.

I stayed in the tent for at least seven years. By then, I replaced the original tent at least three times and had a box spring and a full-size mattress in there. I Have lived in my tent alone and at peace, without having to deal with any confusion and drama from others until I was able to focus on writing and selling my book Homeless lives Matter, Homeless My story and make enough money to move into a decent place.

Principles and morals:

One of the lessons I learned, is that I have to have some kind of principles that guide the way I live and conduct myself. I understand that everything I do, have consequences and effects that can be positive or negative. Many times folks asked me whether I believe in God or Jesus or the bible.

I was selling my book as usual and an elderly couple walking down towards the Washington monument stopped right in front of me. There were in town for a pro-life march. Pro-life means anti-abortion in American pollical jargon. The husband, asked me, " Will I find Jesus in this?" He was talking about my book. I had few seconds to think very fast of the appropriate answer to give him. "Yes," I said. I am Jesus and if you get my book you are doing what Jesus asked you to do. I rushed to explain myself for fear that he might misunderstand my statement. I explained to him that I was referring to bible verses where Jesus said that he will deny entrance into paradise to those who see a poor man in need and do not help him, because the poor man is him. So, I use Jesus' own logic to explain to the main that the homeless are Jesus and they deserve to be assisted and helped by those who believe in Jesus.

I am saying this to say that what is important to me is the principles that all religions including Christianity share across the board. Don't steal, don't kill, don't lie, don't do wrong to others are universal principles that all humans should know instinctively. Those principles are inscribed in the DNA of all of us human beings.

I do not subscribe to any particular belief system but I agree that I should have morals and principles no matter whether I adhere to a belief or faith or religion or not. This is the mindset I operate from and lived by even with my imperfections.

Empathy

When I used to sell my books on the street and nobody stopped to buy a copy after a couple of hours, I used to get very upset, but to calm myself down, I was saying to myself" Leo, nobody owes you anything, you just got to do something different to attract more customers."

I don't think a person is wrong for not giving to every beggar on his path. But at the same time, I believe in having empathy. Empathy means to be able to feel sad or concerned about somebody else plight and feel the desire to help that person or say or do anything to make him or her feel better. A person who has empathy cannot simply ignore the pain and suffering of others. This is one of the principles I have grown to embrace on a deeper level because I was destitute and was reduced to a beggar speaking. The only difference with other homeless beggars around me was that I was selling something, which was copies of my book instead of just shaking a cup. Before I became homeless myself, I was not feeling sorry for beggars all the time. Sometimes, I just passed them without feeling any compassion for them. But being in their shoes made me feel different. This is why I am telling you to put yourself in somebody's shoes, which means to mentally imagine yourself being in the same situation as them. I am sure you would like others to understand what you are going through and help you out instead of just ignoring you.

Being homeless myself and being around homeless people most of the time, made me more able to feel the pain of being destitute, and being into a state of mental, emotional, and physical suffering. But you don't have to be poor, homeless, or in emotional, mental, and physical suffering to have empathy. You should feel the pain of others as if it was you in that situation because if it was you, most likely, you would like others to empathize with your situation. Imagine you see a person walking by you and grab their chest and fall on the ground and become and become motionless. Would you assist them by calling emergency service, or will you keep on going by your business because you don't feel like stopping, because if you do, you will miss your bus about to pull up in one minute? Now, if it was you in that situation, would like a person you just walked by . to ignore you because he has a bus to catch and don't want to stop and check on you and get you some help although you just had a heart attack in front of him or her?

So many times, I walked down the streets and saw somebody on the ground and folks walked by that person without checking on them to know whether they were just drunk, or sick and in urgent need of help. Anytime I walk by a person laying on the sidewalk, and looking like they are not ok, I stop and check on them and ask them if they are ok and if they want me to call for help.

Whenever you see a person who looks like they may need some help, don't ignore them. Pull your phone out and call emergency even if you do not feel like approaching them and ask them if they are ok. Do that because if it is you having a seizure, getting sick, passing out, or being stacked by someone else, I bet you, you will want anyone seeing you in a distressful situation, to assist you or call for help. You would not want anyone witnessing you being attacked to simply ignore you.

I know most of the time, we see a person attacked by another person and we don't want to get involved, either because we are afraid the attacker or attackers may retaliate against us. Or sometimes we just want to mind about business because we feel like we got nothing to do with what is happening in front of our very eyes. I have seen men abusing women in public and people turn their eyes away as if they did not see that guy slap that that girl or that younger man punched that older guy. Because I have been homeless for a long time, I have seen so many incidents like that when folks constantly attack others in public and nobody says or does anything to assist the person getting hurt. One night, I was walking up the street to the bus stop and I saw a younger man outside of a store threatening another guy a little older than him. He was asking the guy to pay him some money he owed him. When the guy came up the store, he started stabbing him with a knife. I tried to get as far as possible from the scene to call 911 or flag a police car and direct them to the scene. But before I had a chance to make the call, I saw the person who was stabbed walk to the gas station not far from the scene. I told myself, well, he may get the gas station attendant or someone pulling up there for gas, to call 911 or take him to the hospital. But honest truth, I was hesitant to call 911 while I was still near the scene because it was not far from where I catch the bus every night and where I used to go take a shower in the morning. Whoever did the stabbing seems to be someone who was frequently present in the vicinity.

So, I don't understand why sometimes, people witness violent attacks and are hesitant to call for help. But, in situations when there is no need to fear for your safety or your life, you should not hesitate to assist or seek help for any person in distress.

Compassion is also a principle that I value because it is an expression of empathy. When you have compassion, you can feel the desire to see other people overcome the bad situation they are in and willing to help them out however you can. Maybe it is not the correct way to express it, but to express it simply, to have compassion is to feel sorry for people going through a hard time. Empathy is more than compassion because it is the ability to not just feel sorry for people but to be able to feel their situation as if it was yours.

I will give an example. A woman came to me while I was selling my book as usual, and asked me if she could pray for me. I told her, that it was no problem. I needed all the prayers I could get. " Lord, I want you to forgive him whatever he did wrong in his life that caused you to allow such a punishment on him" was one of the lines in her prayer. I do not understand why some people want to guilt a person suffering as if everybody going through a hard time deserves their predicament. And she was not the only person who came to me with prayers like that. A couple of times, when people told me that I needed to repent so that God will forgive me and take me out of homelessness, I tell them that everybody goes through situations that they did not necessarily cause. I always asked them if they are familiar with the story of Job in the Bible and then I teach them about that story. Sorry, I don't want to sound religious here. Honest truth, I am an agnostic which means that when it comes to religion, I am totally confused. I am not an atheist but I do not have a clear understanding of God and everything about religion. I just don't know and I am comfortable not knowing because I am seeking knowledge. I want to understand God and religion, not through faith but knowledge. So, back to the story of Job. He was a righteous and pious man who was a friend of God and never did anything wrong. He was a wealthy and well-respected man in his community. One day the devil went to a meeting that God was having with his children according to the bible. He convinced God to accept a bet that if he, the devil is allowed by God to torment Job, he will curse God and stop worshipping him. God accepted the bet and allowed the devil to do anything to Job but not kill him. Job was afflicted by the devil who took everything from him and gave him a bad illness. Job became so poor that everybody in the town started making fun of him. He was now a sick and beggar. His wife told him to curse God, he refused. But here is the intriguing part of the story that I always focus on when I share it with the folks asking me to repent so that I will no longer be homeless. Job friends came to him and said the same thing to him. "You are in this predicament because you committed a bad sin. There is no way God will allow you to be in such a mess unless you did something wrong and he punished you". Job looked at his friends in the eyes and told them that he did not do anything to deserve his afflictions and that he will repeat the same thing in God's face. His friends accused him of blasphemy and departed from him. But God went to his friends and told them that they were wrong and Job was right, he was just being tested. The story ends with God restoring Job to his previous status by blessing him with more wealth than he had before.

I use that story to make folks understand that sometimes bad things happen to people. Sometimes people just have bad luck. So, when we have empathy, you do not judge people, you just show compassion for them and put yourselves in their shoes

Now let's talk about apathy. When you have apathy, which is the opposite of empathy, you feel no compassion towards someone in need of help. It is easy to look at others going through hard times and ignore them or judge and condemn them for what they going through. But just imagine for a second that it was you in their shoes, how would you like others to think about you and react towards you?

Don't make assumptions about people's reality based on what you see. You have no idea how much pain, suffering, and unhappiness they are silently going through. What you see can be an illusion. People can look happy but be going through a whole lot and not showing it. Everybody has some type of unhappy or stressful situation they dealing with, that you might have no idea about.

I try to understand people instead of judging them because I want others to understand and not judge me. Let's be compassionate and kind to one another. To me, that is what being righteous means. To be righteous to me, does not mean that you have to be a religious person necessarily. To be righteous means to conduct yourself according to what is right and to be good and do good.

I understand that I am subjected to the laws of nature. I understand that everything in the universe and nature is subjected to laws that create order and harmony. I understand that my life on earth as a human being is possible only because the planet earth itself is rotating around itself in twenty-four hours and moving in a circle around the sun in three hundred and sixty-five days. They are therefore following some natural laws that we call rotation and revolution. All planets in what we call the Solar System gravitates around the sun.

Imagine for instance that the earth decides to move in a different direction instead of its normal course, there will be chaos in our solar system and life on earth will no longer exist.

It does not matter what culture, religion, beliefs, nation, you are part of, they all share the same fundamental universal principles of good versus evil.

All of them forbid taking another human being life, causing physical or emotional harm to another human being; taking anything from another human being, steal, we should not cause harm to others; denying to other human beings; their freedoms and basic rights, and denying assistance and help to other human beings in danger.

Here are some of the principles I try to apply in my life.

Kindness:

I always try to be kind to others and I appreciate it when others are kind to me. I give a lot without expecting anything in return. I just like to see other people happy. I don't like to see anyone going through a hard time. I know what it feels like to needy and not having anything. So, when I can help, I do with no hesitation. But when someone thinks that I am giving because I am stupid and that they think they are taking advantage of my kindness, I just cut them off. Although I have tons of stories about a lot of ingrateful people that I helped while needing help myself, I will write about it. I have received so much from kind people, most of them total strangers. So when I give, it is for me another way of sharing what I receive. While I was homeless and selling my book on the street, I met so many good people who became to me, what I call angels. People that I could always call for assistance. For example, when I needed an address to have copies of my book shipped to me so I could sell them on the street, it was angels who

109

offered that I ship my book to their home or office address and they will bring them to me where I was selling my books at. It was angels that constantly donated to me without me asking.

It was angels who came all the way to my tent or met me somewhere downtown to give me blankets, packs of tuna, boxes of crackers, and many things that were useful once I was staying outside in my tent. So, to me, giving to someone else who is in need like me, is a way of expressing my gratitude to those who gave to me when I needed it.

Honestly:

I like to be as honest as possible when I deal with people to be trusted and not distrusted. People who know me know that I will never go out of my way to deceive them or trying to cheat them. I personally do not like to deal with anybody that I cannot trust. I assume also that nobody would like to deal with me if they cannot trust me. So, I think you should always give people no reason to distrust you. You will reap a greater benefit by being trustworthy than being deceitful. Yes, they are situations where you may need not divulge all your business if it is going to your detriment, or cause you harm. You have to be careful about putting all your business out there. Everything is not for everybody to know. If telling the truth, can cause you embarrassment, shame, emotional distress, pain, suffering, or any other harm, then, keep your business to yourself. Be careful with your sensitive information. Do not reveal them to anyone who may use them to scam you, or impersonate you or use them maliciously to your detriment.

Be honest only to someone you can trust. But do not tell all your business to someone you may have a good reason not to trust. I am quite sure, you will not let a person that you should not trust, use your phone while you are using the bathroom for enough time for them to get on some of your online accounts and do a transaction behind your back. I am sure you will have enough sense to lie to that person by telling him that you need to make an important call on your phone while you are using the bathroom if you do not want to hurt their feelings by telling them no when they ask to use your phone while you are using the bathroom.

If being honest and telling the truth can be used against me to cause me harm or do me wrong, then I will lie to protect myself and will not have any moral issue with that.

If you walk up on a deserted and dark street at night and someone who looks suspicious to you, approach you and ask you if you have change for a twenty-, fifty- or hundred-dollar bill, I am quite sure, you will be smart enough to tell him that you have no money even if you do, so that you will not end up getting robbed.

Sometimes you just have to tell a person a lie in order to avoid hurting their feelings. If a person has a crush on you, but you feel that they are not your type, I am quite sure, you will not hurt their feelings by telling them "Look, you are not my type, I don't find you attractive". I am quite sure you will be nice enough to lie to them that you are not ready for a relationship or something else but the truth that will cause them pain.

It is hard, to be honest, all the time, but I try to be honest when there is no reason to be dishonest and when it is necessary to create trust between me and whoever I trust and expect trust from. I prefer to be trusted than causing people to distrust me by not being honest with them.

Tolerance:

I believe in being tolerant because I have so many imperfections in myself. So how can I expect perfections from others when I expect others to tolerate me? Being tolerant made it easy for me to deal with anybody even at times, with those who get on my nerves, But I am quite sure, I get on a lot of people's nerves as well.

One thing I always do is apologize when I hurt someone's feelings. Even if a person does not accept my apology and wants to hold grudges, I still feel t peace with my conscience because I did my part.

Although I always try to tolerate a person who is doing things that annoy me, I acknowledge that there is a limit when I simply remove myself from the presence or the company of such a person. When you feel annoyed by someone's behavior, there is no need to get into arguments with that person. Just end the situation by stop arguing or just go away from that person. To tolerate does not mean that you got to put up with abuse or violence against yourself. I have said that time and time again to some female friends that I knew on the street.

This particular lady, that I knew twenty-some years ago, used to be in an abusive relationship. She was an alcoholic. I knew her boyfriend as well in the homeless circles. Any time I run through her, she had a black eye or swollen face and lips because her boyfriend had beat her up during their frequent quarrels. I used to warn her that she needed to end that relationship because one day he will give her a fatal blow. The last time I saw her, she was wearing a cast on her arm because her boyfriend had broken her arm. I told her again to get out of that relationship. She swore to me that she would never go back to him again. The next thing I know, she went back until one day, someone told me that she was in a coma after her boyfriend beat her. I have never seen or heard of her again. That was about twenty years ago.

When I talk about tolerance, I am not talking about allowing others to abuse you because you try to understand and forgive them. Please get out of any domestic violence you may find yourself in. You should not love anyone abusing you more than you love yourself. By tolerance, I don't mean to keep yourself in a relationship that is dysfunctional and in which there is no peace but only arguments and violent interactions.

By tolerance, I mean, accepting people as they are and see in them the same humanity as ours and not treating them with contempt or hate because they don't look like us, they don't believe in what we believe, they don't share the same culture as us, or they are just different from us.

One of my issues with intolerance, the opposite of tolerance, is that it is so present within religion. This is why when people trying to discuss with me whether I share their beliefs, I try to avoid such conversation because they might not tolerate any view I may have that diverges from theirs.

Remove yourself from a negative environment and people

I always try to reflect positive energy inside me and around me so that I can turn bad luck into good luck and enemies into friends. When I am in an environment or around people and I feel a negative vibe, I remove myself from there. If people want to be negative, act negative and talk negative, that is their right, but I get away from that. I don't mind being by myself unless I am in the company of kind, respectful and good people.

Do not do things that will make people hate me, be uncomfortable to be in your presence, or have nothing good to say about you but warn others to stay away from you. I like when I walk up the street or in a park and see a group of folks and one in their midst recognizing me and telling out loud, "this is my man Leo, good dude. Very nice dude ", and then everybody looks at me as if they were just introduced to a nice person. I know you don't like it when you show up in public, everybody starts scattering because nobody wants to be in your company. And in your back, everybody has nothing good to say about you but stuff that" This dude or this lady ain't right! Don't mess with him or her. He or she is trouble." Make it so that even a stranger coming into your presence feels good vibes from you. It is not what you do, it is how you do it. I know you heard that before. Conduct yourself in a way that attracts people towards you and does not repulse them. What I am basically saying is that, don't be an asshole. Don't talk to people or act towards them in a rude and condescending and disrespectful manner.

Create a peaceful environment around you. It cost you nothing to treat others with respect and be friendly. Being nice and respectful will attract good people towards you.

CHAPTER 7

That I have to be healthy

One of the lessons I have learned from surviving through hard times is that I need to be healthy all the time, not just physically but mentally as well.

No matter how difficult the life I was living was, I always tell myself this; Take care of yourself, I mean your body and your mind in order to live or survive on this earth. If you don't, your body and your mind will not be working properly, you will get sick and go through a lot of pain and suffering. You got to take care of your health because it is worth more than all the riches and possessions you may have or may strive for. I am giving you the same advice as well. No matter what is going on with your life, please do not neglect your health. Yes, your health can be compromised accidentally, inadvertently, or by situations beyond your control. But as long as you can prevent and avoid situations that will jeopardize your health, please do so.

Feed yourself with the right food:

If you are capable of affording food, then make sure you feed yourself with the right food that your body needs to stay healthy and not get sick. If you are too poor to afford the right food for yourself and have to rely on charity or others or the government to have access to food, then try to get the best of what you are given. I cannot tell you what to eat because you are going to eat what you like. And besides, I am not a doctor. But I know one thing, your body will let you know how it feels about what you ingest whether it is food or not. Therefore you should take interest in knowing what you eat. Yes, the food you eat may taste very good, but how much good and how much harm it does to your body? You should always be curious to know and not just be content with the taste of what you eat. There are people out there only concerned about making money by selling you food and I am talking here about big corporations and food manufacturers. Many if not most of them are not concerned about how the food they manufacture and sell impacts your body. All they are concern about is making a big profit from the goods they sell you. You are the one who should care about what you eat.

Have you ever taken the time to look at the list of content on any packaged food you buy in the store? I always do that and end up putting the stuff back on the shelf, because it is hard for me to read all the names of all these chemicals added to the food to preserve it, knowing that all these will end up in my body and cause it more harm than good. When you go to the store, have you ever wondered why you see the same fruits in two different sections? Some fruits and vegetables marked as organic and more expensive than the others which are most likely genetically modified by food producers and big corporations so they can grow faster and bigger?

I am not here to badmouth food producers and corporations. I am just here to tell you to be careful what you consume as food because when you get sick from ingesting all these chemicals, it is not going to be fun. It is a friend of mine who I met when we were homeless. He finally got his place when he got sick. Anytime I meet him, he is on his way to or from the medical facilities where he goes regularly for dialysis. His kidneys are messed up and not working properly. They have to stick big needles in his arms and have him sit in a chair or on a bed for hours while his blood is diverted into a machine that cleans it of particles and excess fluids that the kidney normally removes from the blood when it works perfectly. My friend's harm is so deformed because of the procedure he goes through twice a week I think.

Be careful about all the processed food that you ingest. Your body may not process them very well. They might end up hurting your vital organs like your blood, your kidneys, your liver, and even your heart. When I was homeless and poor, I had no place to cook my own food. So, I had to rely on preserved food, mostly canned. But since I was able to have a place, I had been buying fresh vegetables, fruits, and fish and sometimes but rarely, some poultry, and cook my own meal.

When I was living in a tent, I tried not to go to the soup kitchens as much because, most of the breakfast there had processed meat in them, like sausage and bacon. And a lot of the lunch had hotdogs. I am not vegetarian but I try not to eat processed meat. I am not telling you not to eat processed meat. I am only telling you that I chose not to eat processed meat because I thought I will be healthier eating something else than processed meat, which include Sausages, hot dogs, salami, ham, cured bacon, salted and cured meat, corned beef, smoked meat, dried meat, beef jerky, and canned meat.

I have seen so many people in the homeless community suffer from high blood pressure, stroke, heart attack, Kidney failure, diabetes, and cancer. Smoking cigarettes, drinking alcohol, and shooting drugs may be the reason why those diseases are prevalent in poor communities including the homeless community. But, I am quite sure processed food is most certainly also impacting negatively the health of poor people whose diet is more likely to be based on processed food. I am not an expert on these issues, but I have always been careful of what I eat because, as a poor and homeless person who saw too many sick friends, I understood that the food we are exposed to, affects our health.

But here is an excerpt of an article titled; The many health risks of processed food, from the website Laborer's Health and Safety Fund of North America, that explains better than I can what processed food is and what its impact on your health is:

May 2019; Vol 15, Num 12

The Many Health Risks of Processed Foods

What Is Processed Food?

Processed food is any food that's altered during preparation to make it more convenient, shelf-stable or flavorful. ...Most foods we eat have been processed in some way by the time they reach our plates. However, the concern about processed food isn't over items like canned tomatoes or canned tuna, which are processed to lock in freshness and nutrients. The concern is over more heavily processed foods like crackers, jarred pasta sauces and cake mixes. And we eat a lot of these foods – it's estimated that more than half the calories in the average American diet come from ultra-processed foods.

Source: American Institute for Cancer Research

Health Risks of Heavily Processed Foods

There are many potential health effects of ultra processed foods, including:

Too much sugar, sodium and fat. Heavily processed foods often include unhealthy levels of added sugar, sodium and fat. These ingredients make the food we eat taste better, but too much of them leads to serious health issues like obesity, heart disease, high blood pressure and diabetes.

Lacking in nutritional value. Heavy processing strips many foods of their basic nutrients, which is why many foods today are fortified with fiber, vitamins and minerals.

Calorie dense and addicting. It's very easy to overindulge in unhealthy food and consume more calories than we realize.. Processed foods are also designed to stimulate our brain's "feel-good" dopamine center, making us crave more. of them in the future.

Quicker to digest. Processed foods are easier to digest than unprocessed, whole foods. That means our bodies burn less energy (hint: calories) digesting them. It's estimated we burn half as many calories digesting processed foods compared to unprocessed foods. This fact combined with the calorie density of processed foods in general can make it easy to pack on the pounds.

Full of artificial ingredients. There are about 5,000 substances that get added to our food. Most of them have never been tested by anyone other than the company using them. That includes additives to change color, texture, flavor and odor as well as ingredients like preservatives and sweeteners.

Reducing Processed Foods in Your Diet

Even if you wanted to, it would be very difficult to remove all heavily processed foods from your diet. That would mean not eating out at most restaurants and skipping that hot dog at the family barbeque. However, there are many things you can do to reduce the amount of processed food you consume:

Check the label. The longer the ingredient list, the more processed a food is. If most of the ingredients are hard-to-pronounce chemicals instead of actual food, it's a safe bet that food is heavily processed.

Shop the outside aisles at the grocery store. The center aisles of most grocery stores are full of packaged items and ready-made foods that are heavily processed. Aim to buy more foods from the produce and dairy aisles.

Opt for minimally processed meats. Choose meats that have been minimally processed (e.g., seafood, chicken breast) while avoiding heavily processed meats (e.g., sausage, cured meats like bacon).

Start slowly. It's okay to slowly replace processed foods in your diet with more fresh foods. In fact, it may make you more likely to stick to these changes long-term.

Cook more meals at home. You might not always be in control of your diet while traveling, but you are at home. Make your own frozen meals by cooking a larger batch and freezing the leftovers, or whip up your own salad dressing.

119

While many aspects of our health can be complicated, eating less processed food doesn't have to be. When in doubt, just start with real food." (source: https://www.lhsfna.org/index.cfm/lifelines/may-2019/the-many-health-risks-of-processed-foods /)

I will tell you no lie, I love corned beef and could not help to get a corned beef can from time to time when I was staying in my tent. But most of the time, mainly during the Coronavirus shutdown and quarantine, I used to buy a supply of tuna fish can and eat it with crackers most of the time or some bread sometimes.

But, my whole thing about food in moderation. Everything you need, processed or not can harm you if you too much of it. Even too much water can be harmful to certain people. You have to know your body and what it needs more and less.

I eat according to certain needs and desires for my body. For example, when I feel my thighs are rubbing against one another, it means my body is gaining more weight than I feel comfortable carrying around. The last time I was at the doctor's, I weighed 274 pounds. That was too much for me. I never weighed that much. I decided to eat less meat and consumed less sugar. I started consuming more water and less soda or sweetened carbonated drinks. I still was addicted to fruit juices, but I had to adjust to drinking water, which I was not very good at doing. I had to force myself to drink water.

If you drink too much alcohol, whether it is beer, wine, or liquor, you already know that too much of it is not good for your body. You are messing up your liver. You already know that. No reason for me to tell you to moderate your use of alcohol. There is nothing wrong with drinking alcohol, but you have to drink in moderation because too much alcohol will intoxicate your body and harm you. Same with drugs and smoking cigarettes. I know once you get addicted to these things, it is hard to just quit. So, I am not here to judge you for what you to get high, but I am only encouraging you to moderate the use of anything that can intoxicate your body or cause it harm in the long run.

I am insisting that you do what you need to do to be in good health because from my experience surviving outside as a homeless, I can assure you that being in good health help you survive and deal with tough situations better. I have been in relatively good health living outside in a tent with little money. Being in good health helped me survived better under harsh conditions. When you look at the picture on the cover of my book Homeless Lives Matter, Homeless My story, you see almost buried in the snow. Actually, I took that picture maybe a week after half of the snow surrounded the tent, melted. But, when we had that snowstorm in Washington DC and the DC Government sent crews out there to pick all homeless and take them to a warming center, and when all the streets were shut down by the snow, I was inside that tent for two straight days. At one point I was thirsty and could not sip a drop of water out of a frozen gallon bottle of water I had with me. But overall, I was alright. Many times I slept in the freezing cold with everything turning into ice around and inside my tent.

I was able to survive the scorching heat and the subzero cold, sleeping outside in a tent at age fifty because I was in good health. Or because I made sure I was in good health shall I rather say. Because you are going through a hard time is not an excuse to neglect your health. You do not have to seek refuge in alcohol or gluttony. It was a time when I would eat a lot of junk food simply because I was stressed out. Don't do it. I ended up weighing 274 pounds and was still homeless. Anytime I run through someone I had not seen in a long time, the first thing they will say out of their mouth was" You getting big". That did not sound like a compliment to me. It sounded to me like, watch your weight.

Honest truth, I used to stop at the Safeway store on New York and 5th street North West, Washington DC, every night on my way to my tent after selling my book, and get some oatmeal pies, some either grapefruit of apple juice or some lemonade. I use to eat the entire box of oatmeal pies or sometimes some Madeleine and drink the entire bottle of juice during the night. I normally used to get to my tent anytime between midnight and 2 am. This is what happened one night, just to digress a little bit. I had finished selling my book. It was around 11 pm. I went to the 24-hour Safeway as usual. I already had some tuna cans in my tent. I only needed some to eat it with. I don't remember whether I got some potato salad or some bread or some crackers. I always get one of the three and eat it with one or two tuna cans, depending on how hungry I am. I got to my tent about an hour later. Did I walk? Did I ride my bike? I can't remember. But I know that I was very tired when I got into my tent. I ingurgitated my food as fast as possible and laid on the bed and fell asleep. In the middle of my sleep, as I always used to do, I grabbed the box of oatmeal pies, opened it in the dark with my eyes closed and grabbed a couple of the pies, and ate them while half asleep, and went back to sleep. I think I only ate a couple of them. There are 8 of them in the box. I think it was about 4 or 5 am when I tried to grab a couple more while still sleeping. It was still dark. I felt around the bed but could not find the box. I used a flashlight and looked all over the bed. Nothing. I guessed that the box fell off the bed. I directed the flashlight towards the bottom side of the bed and guess what I saw. You won't believe it. Some bright eyes by a box of copies of my book. It was a raccoon who was having a feast with my oatmeal pie. I run out of that tent like a little girl because I realized that I had a serious problem that I needed to get rid of right away. I had lived in that tent and other tents in the same spot for few years and some of the animals I never wish to find in my tent were raccoons, possums, and snakes. I had field mice coming in sometimes but I never got bothered by them. But raccoons? Hell no, it had to go. I am here talking about health. I know raccoons carry rabies. I mean some of them. I did not want to get bit or scratch a raccoon and catch rabies. I was trying so hard to stay healthy. Now I had an uninvited and unwanted guess in my tent about to give me rabies. Sorry Mister Raccoon, you had to go. I know you animal rights guys will say to me, hey Leo, you were in their natural environment. I understand all that, but he or it didn't have to come inside my tent. He could hand around but not come inside. Well, I had food in there, I know. I understand, but I had to get it out of there. I didn't care about the oatmeal pies. He ate everything anyway because the box was empty. I ate two, he ate 6 of the oatmeal pies. I grabbed a metal bar I kept in the tent for protection. I only wanted to scare him and never hurt him. So I went outside the tent and just hit on the side of the tent from the outside in order to force it to the door of the tent, but to no avail. It kept moving from one side of the tent to another. I grabbed the mattress pulled it out, did the same with the mattress box, and turned the tent around. It got out and did not go too far. It climbs a tree and stayed in it. It was moving very slow. I did have a hole in the tent because the tent was torn. That is probably how it got in it that easy. Hen I left the morning to go take my shower at SOME, I covered the hole. I stayed out all night, working on my laptop outside. When I returned early in the morning around 6:00 am, I was not worried about the raccoon. It was not in the small tree that he had climbed in the previous day. I opened my tent, but guess who was in there? The Raccoon. I had a plastic basket at the entrance of the tent. It was cozy in there. I was sleepy and I needed my tent by myself. So, I got him out and chased it all the way to the bridge by the spot where I keep my trash. I felt like the trash will be something it would want to consider checking. I am quite sure they were some leftover food in there. I had another situation a year or two before with a strayed cat. I have nothing against cats whatsoever. But, I was born with severe asthma and suffered from it all my childhood until I was fortunate to get rid of it around age 16. But, asthma is probably one of the worse illnesses if you ask me. To not be able to breathe is very disturbing. I grew up having severe asthma. You can therefore imagine how it feels to not have that issue anymore. The illness disappeared from my body miraculously. I was born very sick and grew up out of that sickness. But, I still have asthma-like attacks and episodes when I am exposed to some animal hair and especially cats. I get extremely sick, out of breath and my chest gets so heavy when I am exposed to cat hair. This is why I cannot have a cat in proximity or their hair on a surface that I come in contact with. One day, I stepped out of my tent and saw a cat coming out of the woods not far away. I don't know what took me, I had some food, and toss it at it. The next thing I know, I was resting in my tent the next day, a Sunday if I remember. I heard the cat meowing outside of the tent. I did not have a problem give it some food but not too close to my tent. So, I grabbed some food and walked towards the woods, and tossed it over there. Later on, it came back meowing again. I ignored it. The next day, I came back from downtown, and guess what I saw? The cat in my bed. I got worried that my health was being in jeopardy because now I had to worry about the cat's hair in my bed. I chased it out of the tent and run after it all the way to the woods just to scare it enough so that it would not return inside the tent when I am absent. But I did not harm it besides scarring it.

It never returned. I know many of you have cats as pets and may not like the fact that I chased that cat away from my tent. Some of you may say, how can you be homeless and have no empathy for a homeless cat? I know how feel, but I hope you know how I felt. It was about my health. I could not afford to put my health in danger by sharing my tent with a raccoon or a cat. I love animals, don't get me wrong. But, I cannot just share my tents with animals who could give me a serious disease. I would not even share my tent with a human being who will give me Covid or Tuberculosis or any infectious disease. So, this is just a matter of common sense. You got to use common sense to protect yourself against any disease that will put your life in danger.

We take chances sometimes and exposes ourselves to dangerous diseases mostly when it comes to sex. Sometimes we are so consumed with the desire to gratify ourselves that we purposely do not protect ourselves when having sex. And then we end up with sexually transmitted disease knowing some of them like HIV or Herpes or Hepatitis, have no cure and can kill us. I know condom is not comfortable, but, if you can, please wear one. Sorry for getting into your business but we got one life to live, let's live it healthy and protect it from diseases that can harm or kill us.

I also understood that a way to stay healthy was to take care of my hygiene which to me starts with washing my body every day without exception. If you live in a house and have running water and a shower, why would not shower? I don't understand that. I have lived in places with people that never got into the shower ever. They will go as far as using a rag and wash their face, body, and genital parts at the sink, but will never let the water run over their body. I don't understand why anybody would be afraid of water. This is crazy. Please take a shower. At least twice a day. Just joking. At least twice a week. Do you have any idea of how many bacteria crawl on every part of your body? Billions of them. Dirt piles on your skin every second although you may not see it. Your body does not need water only on the inside, it also needs water to wash the outside. Up to 60 percent of your body is water. Water is ok, don't be scare of it. It cleanses you and makes you healthier inside and outside.

 I slept outside in a tent for years but guess what, I always make sure I shower at least once a day. Being homeless was not an excuse good enough for me not to figure a way to shower. I normally rode my bike or walked down the street on North Capitol Street to a place called SOME to shower. I had to make it there very early before 7 am to be sure to make it on the shower list before the covid Pandemic. During the Covid Pandemic, folks who wanted to take a shower just lined up outside the entrance door and the guy doing showers came outside to call the next one in when a shower was available. I stopped going to SOME or to any crowded place when the COVID Pandemic started. I just figure a way to shower at my camp by my tent. I went out late at night went the streets were empty and the stores were less crowded and got me at least two bottles of 1-gallon water and took it to my tent to use to shower in the morning. But, I also had one or two persons bring me a supply of water at my tent so that I had enough water to last me for at least a week. I also spread some tarp on the grass and recycled some rainwater that I filtered and used to shower and wash my clothes outside my tent. I also had another spot where I went to shower at night. It was by a church downtown. There was a faucet on the side of the church. I stashed a bucket, a bottle of body wash, a washcloth, and a towel in the bushes around that church. I went there almost every night and showered on the side of that church. The streets were empty because everybody was in quarantine. The city had completely shut down. I felt totally fresh and rejuvenated after taking a shower once every day. I felt healthier as well.

I also stashed my dirty clothes in the bushes. Many homeless who slept upstairs in front of the church entrance doors, stashed their belongings in the same bushes. Whenever I needed to wash clothes, I took them from the plastic bag stashed in the bushes and took them to the laundromat on 11th and Rhode Island Avenue.

I normally stayed healthy during the time I was sleeping outside in a tent when I was homeless. I only got sick because of pollen allergies. Other than that, maybe a few migraines here and there, but no serious illness in the last past ten years except the following cases.

One thing I do now that I am no longer homeless is to tie a shopping cart in the back of my bike and put groceries and laundry or even books in the back when I need to carry them with me either from the grocery store, to and from the laundromat or to the post office. I don't know why I never thought about doing the same when I was homeless. When you do not have a place to leave or not stable, or going through a lot, you cannot think right. That was my case. Things that I am doing the right way now, I could not think of doing it right then when I did not have a normal place to live.

I used to pack up my books in an army duffel bag, and carry it on my bag and ride for 45 minutes downtown. I carried probably about 60 pounds on my back every. I used to simply stash the books inside the bushes by the church that I talked about earlier. One time I stashed a box with 100 books wrapped in a big black trash bag in there. One day the folks cleaning the downtown area and working for an organization called DC Downtown services, came and cleaned up the bushes and threw all the homeless people's stuff away. One homeless guy who used to sleep up the stairs in front of the church knew that OI had my books stashed there. He called me and told me that the Downtown folks threw all our stuff away. And that they probably took my books to their office. I rushed downtown and headed to their office next to the McDonald on 13th and New York Avenue. When I got there, I saw a couple of copies of my book on a couple of desks. I told the gentleman in the office about my books. He called the guy who headed the crew that cleaned up the previous afternoon. I asked why were copies of my book on a couple of people's personal desks in that office. Obviously, somebody came with my books in that office and distributed a few to whoever staff that wanted it. Some of the staff kept a copy on their desk. The guy in the office went in the back and collected about 8 copies. I told him that I had a box containing a hundred books. He told me that the guy that he called and who was in charge of the crew that clean the bushes by the church, told him that the only copies that they brought to the office were the ones that the guy in the office collected. But they threw away the rest of the books because they were allegedly rain damaged. I don't that was some bullshit. I tied up the box in two plastic bags. I have been keeping books in those bushes for months and never had any issue with them getting wet despite heavy rain downpours on many occasions. My guess is that they shared the books among themselves and one of them took the rest home. These folks knew that I was selling those books on the streets. So, I suspect one of them thought he could make money from the books someway somehow.

But to make a story short, I stopped stashing my books in those bushes after that incident. I used to sell my books on the street for ten dollars a copy. The one hundred copies that I lost were about one thousand dollars that I could have made but that I lost. I was devastated but that is life.

From then and on, I started carrying my books from my tent to downtown and from downtown to my tent. I used to catch the bus on my way back in because I did not like riding uphill which I had to do all the way from downtown to my tent.

By doing that every day, I started feeling some pain in my right shoulder one day. I thought the pain will last for few days, but it got worse every day to the point when it becomes unbearable. The pain started extending from the right side of my neck to my entire shoulder to the lower part.

I could not sleep because I was in pain all night. I was in pain all day as well. I went to the clinic and the doctor prescribed me some Motrin 800. It did not do me any good. I return to the clinic a few days later. I was prescribed some pills that were supposed to be more effective for shoulder pain. It was expensive but I got it. When I read the warning on the pack, I decided that I would not take it. The warnings said that the medication can cause heart problems and more danger to some other vital organs. Those warnings were not even the side effects. I did not even care to read the side effect. The doctor sent me to a chiropractor, who also told me that I had to take the medication prescribed by the other doctor. But he prescribed a gel form of the same medication. The warnings were the same on the box. I decided to simply endure the pain until it goes away on its own. I went through it for an entire month before the pain slowly evanesced.

I believed that the pain in my shoulder was caused by both me being exposed to the cold since I was sleeping outside in a tent during the winter and also me carrying a heavy load on my bag every day.

Last winter, I decided not to ask a friend who also was homeless but who got a place, whether I could come and stay there the nights when it was too cold outside. He agreed. I gave him twenty dollars every night I went there when I felt like it was too cold to stay in my tent. I did not want to experience the same shoulder pain ever again. Worse pain ever.

The more time I spent staying indoors at my friend's place, the more I was able to cook the type of meals I deemed healthy. What I used to do and am still doing is to google the health benefits of some of the vegetables, fruits, and food products that I was interested in eating. For example, I was a little concerned about my weight, and my vision. So I would google the type of food that has the proper nutrients that will deal with weight or sight for example.

I advise you to spend few minutes on your phone or your computer researching the health benefits or some of the weird stuff you see in the grocery store and see if you may want it. That is what I do. To me, the best medicine is the food you consume, which can also be the worse hazard to your health. Watch what you consume as food. I know if you are poor like me and can only afford McDonald's food, you may end up eating Mc Double or McChicken sandwiches with French fried or chicken nuggets and a cup of Soda as your main daily diet. There is nothing wrong to eat a sandwich from time to time. But, you need to diversify your diet.

One thing I learned while researching on the best food for my eyesight and my weight concern and other concerns as I am getting older, is that the color of fruits and vegetables have different health benefits. As I am typing this now, I just finished my dinner. Guess what I had? I cooked some rice (white) with a stew made of fish, kale greens (green), purple Cabbage (purple), radish (red), habaneros peppers (red and orange), peanut butter (brown). And I peeled about ten limes put them in a blender with some water and filtered the juice and added some honey to make lemonade.

This article titled the importance of a colorful diet explained expertly why a colorful food diet is something you may consider to stay in good health from what you eat.

I got this article titled 5 shades of nutrition from the website of All American Healthcare.

5 SHADES OF NUTRITION

Fitting in all of your essential vitamins and nutrients may be easier than it appears. Just use the rainbow as your guide.

Colorful fruits and veggies contain an abundance of health benefits to the entire body and overall health. Packed with vitamins and nutrients, these foods will give your body the nutrients it needs to function properly and keep you feeling good.

In addition to natural colored fruits and veggies, colored herbs are also good for your health. Below, we have outlined your five shades of nutrients!

1. RED

Red is a strong color of life that can be symbolic of your heart and arteries. A lot of red fruits and veggies serve as a great source for heart health and can help prevent heart disease. Juicy tomatoes, sweet strawberries, crispy red peppers and spicy red cayenne peppers are just a few of the foods in this red hot color. Red fruits and veggies are filled with vitamin C, vitamin A, and lycopene.

Vitamin C can be found in a variety of fruits and vegetables and is commonly used to support the immune system and heart health.

Lycopene, a natural chemical that gives food a red color, is used to prevent heart disease, keep your arteries healthy, help with skin protection, and contains fiber to help with your digestive tract. Tomatoes are an abundant source of lycopene, but it is also found in watermelons, pink grapefruits, apricots and pink guavas.

Red fruits and veggies are also a great source of vitamin A, which helps support your immune system and vision. Vitamin A is made up of retinoids (found in animal foods) and carotenoids (found in plants). The carotenoids also serves as an antioxidant and anti-inflammatory.

Red herbs and spices like cinnamon and ground red pepper are also good for your health. Cinnamon spices are known to have anti-oxidant, anti-diabetic, anti-septic and anti-inflammatory properties. Cinnamon spice may contain the highest anti-oxidant strength of all food sources in nature. On the other hand, ground red pepper is a great source for vitamins and essential minerals such as iron, copper, zinc, potassium, magnesium, vitamin B and selenium.

2. ORANGE

Orange as a color represents an abundance of strength and life, and foods this color can help you feel the same way! Tangerines, carrots, pumpkins, peaches, guavas, sweet potatoes, papayas, mangoes, apricots and oranges all fall under the orange spectrum of the food rainbow. Orange fruits and veggies provide a wide range of health benefits and are a good source of vitamin A, vitamin C, fiber, and beta-carotene.

Beta-carotene is the best known nutrient in orange foods, and serves as the powerful antioxidant that gives sunny, yellow and orange fruits and veggies their bright color. Beta-carotene, a vitamin A retinoid, is good for eye health and anti-aging. Vitamin A is a strong antioxidant that neutralizes free radicals in the body, especially in the eyes.

range fruits and veggies are also stock full of vitamin C, another strong antioxidant which boosts the immune system and protects against cardiovascular disease.

Turmeric, the element that makes mustard bright yellow, a spice commonly used in curry that is filled with health benefits for your body and brain.

3. YELLOW

Yellow is another bright color that represents happiness, joy and health. Bright colored fruits and veggies contain flavonoids, lycopene, potassium, vitamin C and vitamin A. Lemons, bananas, yellow peppers, squash, pineapple, and corn are all great examples of this healthful, yellow food group!

Yellow fruits and veggies contain carotenoids and bioflavonoids, water-soluble plant pigments that function as antioxidants. Like other foods containing these compounds, they provide an abundance of health benefits for your heart, vision, digestion and skin.

Yellow herbs, such as goldenseal, can be used as an astringent or antiseptic and if often used to fight the common cold. Dandelion, another yellow herb, is used to assist with weight control, anemia, and indigestion. Ginger is a yellow healing root known to help with nausea, gas and inflammation. Ginger contains beneficial essential oils that help improve digestions and intestinal inflammation.

4. GREEN

Green represents nature, the environment, and wellness! Green fruits and veggies are packed with fiber and beta-carotene. Some of this green group includes kale, collards, broccoli, cucumbers, spinach, kiwis, limes, green peppers and zucchinis.

Green fruits and veggies contain phytochemicals such as lutein and indoles which help lower your risk of certain cancers, improve eye health, and promote healthy and healthy bones. Broccoli is high in calcium and iron for healthy bones while spinach is full of antioxidants and vitamin K.

Green supplements and herbs are also packed with health benefits. Spirulina is a blue-green algae packed with antioxidants, B-vitamins, and nutrients to support your immune system and provide a variety of health benefits. Mint is an herb also contains essential volatile oils that effect cold-sensitive receptors in the skin, mouth and throat. It is also an excellent source of minerals like potassium, calcium and iron.

5. BLUE & VIOLET

This colorful food group gets its color from anthocyanin, a water-soluble pigment that has been linked with antioxidants and anti-aging properties in the body. Depending on its pH level, the pigment may appear red, purple or blue. Some foods that fall into this color spectrum include blueberries, blackberries, plums, beets, grapes, eggplant, and onions.

Blue and purple foods contain lypocene, flavonoids, and vitamins D & K. They help promote bone health, can help lower the risk of certain cancers, improve memory and increase urinary-tract health.

Blueberries are high in fiber, vitamins E & C, and antioxidants. Eating blueberries has been known to improved cholesterol, increased urinary-

tract health, and boost brain activity. Plums, however, are high in vitamin K, which helps promote bone health, and vitamin B, which boosts your immune system, metabolism and heart health. (Source: https://allamericanhealthcare.net/5-shades-of-nutrition/)

I can understand a homeless or poor person who survives on junk food because they cannot afford to purchase healthy food, but I don't understand some of you who eat bowls of cereals, packs of potatoes or corn chips, and packs of noodles, or Mc Donald burgers and fries and drink sodas all day long. You got to add more nutritious food in your diet. All that junk food is packed with sugar and salt and preservatives. Why do you think there are so many people around you suffering from high blood pressure, diabetes, heart attacks, seizures, failed Kidneys, cancers, obesity, and all kind of sickness? It is because they don't eat right, simple as that. Life is already hard, don't make it worse by making yourself sick with what you eat. What I am telling you is what I tell myself every day. When I feel hungry I remind myself that I have to be careful what I eat. So when I go to a store, I tell myself, be careful what you buy, you want to stay healthy, you can't afford to be sick. Sometimes, I will grab a cake, or some soda, or some chips and tell myself, nope, and put it right back. I am not telling you not to eat some junk food from time to time. I am just telling you to eat junk food in moderation. I know you may not know how to cook. That's ok. Learn how to. You will get good at it with time. No big deal. It is a little messy but you got to clean after yourself as you go. It will end up being very fun when you get used to it. The food you cook yourself will take better, trust me. I am quite sure you can fry your own eggs better than McDonald's. I can. Sometimes when I have to, I will get breakfast at McDonald's if there is nothing else on my trajectory. But, that is very rare for me to do that now that I am no longer homeless. Here again, I am not telling you not to eat fast food. I am just telling you to moderate your consumption of processed food if you are able to.

When I was homeless, I didn't have much of a choice but rely on donated food or fast food to feed myself. But now that I can buy and cook my own meal, I am able to eat fast food in moderation. There was a time when I was drinking juices and sodas only and barely any water. Today, I have to worry about going to the clinic to check myself for diabetes.

You have to take care of your physical health off course, but your mental health even more.

Chapter 8

Mental strength

That I have to be strong mentally and emotionally to survive is one of the most important if not the most important lesson I had to learn while going through hell. . I am now seeing the tunnel but the struggle is not over yet.

You have to take care of your mind. With a strong mind, you can overcome so much. So, always make sure you are ok mentally. No joke. If your mind is not right, your life is not going to be alright. I am being real with you.

As I explained in my previous book, Homeless Lives Matter, Homeless My story, one day I was so stressed out, I felt like I was about to lose my mind. I literally started crying. I had just left the shelter in Southwest Washington DC. That was over a decade ago when I used to go to homeless shelters. I have stayed in nearly all the shelters in Washington DC over the last decade, if not more. I felt so terrible about myself. I was totally disgusted about my life. The kind of feeling that may you consider suicide. The last time I attempted suicide, I promised myself that no matter what I go through in life, I will never attempt to take my life. That was 30 some years ago. I explained it in chapter 1. Why am I suffering so much? I asked myself. It seemed like I was just born to suffer from no respite. The psychiatrist that I had seen then had concluded that I was perfectly normal and I did not have any mental illness. Nonetheless, the hardship I was going through for years and years was enough to drive any normal person to insanity. While I was getting emotional about my life miseries and my homelessness, I started worried about my mental health. I was Christian then. My reaction was to make this prayer. "God, you can take everything from me but please do not touch my mind." Was a prayer I made. To me, the greatest fear of being homeless and going through hell was always to become crazy, or mentally ill to use a more appropriate word.

After that moment, I decided to be mentally strong and be careful not to allow my predicament to affect me mentally to the point of losing it.

At that time, I was not spending enough time working. I was too depressed. Most of my days were spent at Martin Luther King Library. It was a hub for the city's homeless. There was a church right next to the Library. They were feeding the homeless there starting at 9:30 am. The homeless nicknamed it, the Nine thirty club. You can imagine where the homeless who had breakfast there ended when the place was closed after breakfast. The library was well airconditioned in the summer and well heated in winter. So, it was a perfect place for the homeless to go and stay until it was time to close.

I had got used to that way of life; go to places where breakfast was served in the morning, then go to the library and read books all day, then head to the shelter in the evening after a stop at the food truck, or stop around noon and walk to SOME, about 30 minutes walk away and return to the library.

One thing I did after that day during which I was so depressed, is to check any book dealing with psychiatry to acquaint myself with various mental illnesses in order to check myself for any abnormal behavior so that I would immediately seek psychiatric help if the need was.

At that time, being broke, homeless, ashamed of myself did not matter as much as how I felt about my mental illness. I have seen many homeless totally deteriorate mentally around me. Some folks who seem to be normal when I first met them, started talking to themselves and neglecting their appearance. So many folks in the shelter were mentally ill. At night, I could barely sleep because, sometimes, there were some homeless next to me talking to themselves all night. Others had extremely poor hygiene. It was obvious that they had not been in a shower for weeks. Sleeping next to them caused me some migraines so many times. The stench coming from their clothes and shoes and socks was unbearable. Going to the shelter every night was depressing. All these caused me to worry about my mental health because I didn't whether they were already crazy before becoming homeless or whether homelessness got them into that state.

Sometimes, I caught myself talking out loud while venting some frustrations. "Leo, you got to be careful. Don't do that. You are going to be crazy if you keep talking to yourself so loud" I told myself. I was worrying too much. Honest truth. Most of the knowledge I gain about mental illnesses allowed me to watch myself, pay attention to my behavior and stop worrying too much.

I want to share this story to stress the importance of taking care of your mental health. I had a friend who used to be homeless but had a place by the time I met her. One day, she asked me to take care of Virginia to a store where she could purchase cartons of cigarettes cheaper than in DC where the price was almost double. When I showed up in front of her building, she came downstairs and told me that she was going upstairs to dress up and get ready. A few minutes later, she walked back out of her building and told me that she had changed her mind because she did not have enough money. I told her, no problem I will buy it for you and you because I just want you to know where the is store and to get there. She responded that she did not want me to buy it for her. "OK" I get it and you pay me back whenever you want. She insisted that she did not want any longer and walked back inside her building. I felt like she wasted my time because I came from my tent after she kept calling me to come and take her to that store in Virginia. So, I just rode my bike all the way across the bridge to Virginia to a gas station that was selling the carton of Newport's cigarettes for very cheap, almost half of the cost of the same thing in Washington DC. I came back about an hour later and called her from the downstairs of her building. She came down all upset while I handed her the carton. She refused her and walked away, then walked back but insisted that I take the money. I told her that if she needed the money for something else, it was no problem. I did not need the money. But she tucked the money in my hand and walked away. A few days later, she saw me in the park and thanked me for getting her the cigarettes. I was a little upset at her because she kept pressing me to take her to Virginia to show her where she could get some cheap cigarette and when I show up after she called me to come and take her there, she switched up on me and get mad at me when I still go and get for her. She looked at me in the eyes and laughed out loud and told, me, "Leo you know I am mentally ill. I am bipolar and I see a psychiatrist. I got mood swings. " I appreciated the fact that she was aware of her mental illness and was not ashamed of talking about it. TO me that was very great. It made me aware of the fact that sometimes we rush to judge people without knowing whether their behavior is just intentional or whether they are suffering from an illness that causes them to behave the way they do. Any time she needed some money for food, she used to call me and I rushed to give it to her outside of her building or at Franklin Park, because I knew she was going through some health issues, physically and mentally. Sometimes I called to check on her and she told me that she had been hospitalized after having some mental episodes. It seems to me that the fact that she was aware of her mental illness and was getting professional help, made her life better. She was always in a happy mood when I saw her.

Unfortunately, there are so many folks especially among people on the street, who have a mental illness but do not want to acknowledge it. They therefore not getting the help they need. Their life is made more difficult because of that. They get offended when you try to get them to understand that they might need professional mental help. Il am not crazy". Survival becomes extremely hard for a person who is not taking care of his or her mental health. I was riding my bike one night in the downtown area a bit off Pennsylvania, not far from the White House. It was about 2 or 3 in the morning. I saw this old homeless lady at the bus stop where she is always with her bags. But this time she was totally naked and was washing her genitals and behind with a washcloth, a bar of soap, and a bottle of water. Obviously she was not well upstairs. Another time, I saw this homeless sleeping in a doorway, throw back a twenty-dollar bill and some food that a couple passing by had set next to him thinking he was sleeping. But he got up and threw gap the money and the food and threw it back in the direction of the man and his wife. Many other times, I have seen that same homeless guy forage through trash cans and garbage to pick up some thrown-away food. One day, I was in Franklin's Park. Folks were giving food away. One guy handed some food to the same homeless guy. The other homeless around him told the man to put the food into the trash can because that is the only way he will get food. He never accepted food handed to him. This is obviously a case of severe mental illness.

There are thousands of mentally ill homeless on the street who are not receiving proper help from mental health professionals. I believe that every city with a large homeless population should have a crew of mental health professionals who goes around their city regularly to check on those who are mentally ill and stay on the street.

I see too many older mentally ill homeless women sleeping on the street and not receiving any help. It breaks my heart.

But mental illness is not just a reality among the poor and the homeless. I am not a specialist in mental health, but I have tried to know about mental illnesses or other mentally or psychologically related disorders to check myself and seek help in case. I am inviting you to do the same, mainly if you are stressed, depressed, or too anxious, or if your behavior is becoming abnormal to yourself or others.

We do things that seem weird, strand, or crazy sometimes, but that does not mean that we are having psychological or mental disorders or illnesses. Here is a document, a bit long but very interesting that summarizes the majority of mental and psychological disorders. Please check it out and get informed so that you can help yourself or help somebody else who may need some serious professional psychological or psychiatric help.

I got this document from the website of Very Well Mind:

Types of mental health issues and illnesses

Mental illness is a general term for a group of illnesses that may include symptoms that can affect a person's thinking, perceptions, mood, or behavior. Mental illness can make it difficult for someone to cope with work, relationships, and other demands. The relationship between stress and mental illness is complex, but it is known that stress can worsen an episode of mental illness. Most people can manage their mental illness with medication, counseling, or both. This page lists some of the more common mental health issues and mental illnesses.

Anxiety disorders

Anxiety disorders are a group of mental health disorders that includes generalized anxiety disorders, social phobias, specific phobias (for example, agoraphobia and claustrophobia), panic disorders, obsessive compulsive disorder (OCD) and post-traumatic stress disorder. Untreated, anxiety disorders can lead to significant impairment on people's daily lives.

Behavioral and emotional disorders in children

Common behavior disorders in children include oppositional defiant disorder (ODD), conduct disorder (CD) and attention deficit hyperactivity disorder (ADHD). Treatment for these mental health disorders can include therapy, education and medication.

Bipolar affective disorder

Bipolar affective disorder is a type of mood disorder, previously referred to as 'manic depression'. A person with bipolar disorder experiences episodes of mania (elation) and depression. The person may or may not experience psychotic symptoms. The exact cause is unknown, but a genetic predisposition has been clearly established. Environmental stressors can also trigger episodes of this mental illness.

Depression

Depression is a mood disorder characterized by lowering of mood, loss of interest and enjoyment, and reduced energy. It is not just feeling sad. There are different types and symptoms of depression. There are varying levels of severity and symptoms related to depression. Symptoms of depression can lead to increased risk of suicidal thoughts or behaviors.

Dissociation and dissociative disorders

Dissociation is a mental process where a person disconnects from their thoughts, feelings, memories or sense of identity. Dissociative disorders include dissociative amnesia, dissociative fugue, depersonalization disorder, and dissociative identity disorder.

Eating disorders

Eating disorders include anorexia, bulimia nervosa, and other binge eating disorders. Eating disorders affect females and males and can have serious psychological and physical consequences.

Obsessive compulsive disorder

Obsessive compulsive disorder (OCD) is an anxiety disorder. Obsessions are recurrent thoughts, images or impulses that are intrusive and unwanted. Compulsions are time-consuming and distressing repetitive rituals. Treatments include cognitive behavior therapy (CBT), and medications

Paranoia

Paranoia is the irrational and persistent feeling that people are 'out to get you'. Paranoia may be a symptom of conditions including paranoid personality disorder, delusional (paranoid) disorder and schizophrenia. Treatment for paranoia include medications and psychological support.

Post-traumatic stress disorder

Post-traumatic stress disorder (PTSD) is a mental health condition that can develop as a response to people who have experienced any traumatic event. This can be a car or other serious accident, physical or sexual assault, war-related events or torture, or natural disasters such as bushfires or floods.

Psychosis

People affected by psychosis can experience delusions, hallucinations and confused thinking.. Psychosis can occur in a number of mental illnesses, including drug-induced psychosis, schizophrenia and mood disorders. Medication and psychological support can relieve, or even eliminate, psychotic symptoms.

Schizophrenia

Schizophrenia is a complex psychotic disorder characterized by disruptions to thinking and emotions and a distorted perception of reality. Symptoms of schizophrenia vary widely but may include hallucinations, delusions, thought disorder, social withdrawal, lack of motivation and impaired thinking and memory. People with schizophrenia have a high risk of suicide. Schizophrenia is not a split personality.

- Anxiety, Stress, Depression:

Now everybody sometimes do things that look crazy to ourselves and to others, or we get stressed the hell out sometimes by things that are not that important. That does not mean that we are crazy or that we are mentally ill. We all get stressed out, anxious, depressed, angry sometimes, or a lot of time. But it is perfectly normal when we deal with a lot. So, I want to share some words of encouragement with you if you are dealing with anxiety, stress, and depression.

I can say without any shame that depression played a role in me experiencing chronic homelessness. I have experienced some behavior similar to some of the disorders listed above, like eating disorders and sleeping disorders, and maybe others. I can't say for sure whether the fact that I behaved the same way as described in those disorders, was because I suffered from them or simply because I reacted so as a way to cope with stress. Many times, when I was anxious or stressed out or depressed, I spent sometimes a couple of days or up to three days sleeping in my tent. I would wake up, go get some to eat and some water and shower, and go back to so sleep. Other times, I kept eating and sleeping and eating and sleeping and having nightmares.

For example when I finished writing my first book, Homeless Lives Matter, Homeless My story, I was very anxious about what to do next. I knew I had to go out on the street and sell copies of the book in order to make enough money to afford a place to leave as I idealized. But, now that the book was finished, I was afraid and anxious because I didn't know how folks were going to react to the book. SO, I did not get it printed right away. I had finished writing it in 2016. But, I waited until 6 months later, in 2017 to publish it. Even after I published it, I waited about three more months before making up my mind to go out there and sell it. All that time, I was just stressed out. I slept most of that time. One day, I just snapped out of that depressed state and went out there and started selling the book on the street until I built enough confidence in myself to make it a daily routine. I never went to see a psychiatrist or a mental health specialist.

I only work on myself by talking to myself in my mind. I spent a lot of time telling myself " Leo, you can do it. Stop worrying, stop being anxious, stop being stressed. Stop sleeping every day and waiting for the next day, and the next day, and the next day and times going back and you still have not gone out and sell the book. Get up and go and go and do it". I convinced myself by keeping talking words of encouragement into my mind." You always going to hear two voices talking to your conscience. One will persuade you to stay depressed, another will dissuade you and try to convince you to do the right thing. Both voices are no other than yourself trying to talk to yourself from both sides, one discouraging you, the other one encouraging you. You may blame the devil but it is up to you to listen to the positive side of you instead of your negative side. Anytime, I get disturbed, upset, afraid, dispirited, pessimistic, I talk myself out of it. This is my first way of dealing with depression and stress and anger and pessimism. I talk myself out of those feelings. You have to try to do the same. Don't let the negative voice keep talking. Stop listening to your negative side, and start listening to your positive side. If your negative voice tells you, this is too hard, I am not doing it. Activate the positive voice and let it say to you, I think I am going to try, I am not going to stress myself and discourage myself. "

Even now, I am still struggling with stress and anxiety and fear and depression and anger at times, depression, but I am doing my utmost best to make progress and deal with those feelings and use them to fuel my ambitions and efforts for improvements instead of allowing them to paralyze and prevent me to move forward. For example, now, I am anxious to finish this book in two weeks. That anxiety and stress make me stay up all night and most of the day working on that book so that I can reach my dateline. I don't let the stress and anxiety make me give up and tell myself, "I still have too much to do and not enough time left, therefore I am not going to keep pushing.": Talk to yourself mentally encourage yourself. When you start feeling discouraged and stressed out about something you are working on, tell yourself "I am not going to give up. I can do it, and I will keep on working on it until I get it done. "When you feel sick and you are not healing as fast as you desire and you are suffering and in pain, do not give up, give having a positive way of thinking, and tell yourself" I am going to keep taking my medicine and do what I need to do to improve my health. I know I am in pain but it will get better. " I told you about the pain in my shoulder. But I did not tell you about the 10 teeth that were pulled out of my mouth during one year about two years ago for me to have a denture. I still went to sell my book right after leaving the dentist's office after each procedure even though I had three or two teeth pulled at a time. It was very depressing to see almost all my natural teeth being pulled away right after the pain in the shoulder that lasted a whole month day and night, I still was outside selling my book while holding my shoulder in acute pain. I mentally ignored the pain and focused on making money because I needed to make money to take care of myself. Even now, I still have another pain in my back that lasted seven years now. It is not a permanent pain but it happens all of a sudden and in the last few seconds. But it is a sharp pain that feels like somebody sticking a long nail inside my back. That pain can happen once a day, or once a week, or ten times a day. I never know when to expect it. But whenever it comes, it makes me scream sometimes. But I am used to being in pain and I deal with it without problem until any doctor can tell me exactly what it is. Now I am concentrated on succeeding in all my endeavors so that I can be self-sufficient and independent and permanently out of poverty. Accomplishing my urgent goals motivates me to not allow stress or pain to slow me down or stop me until I am in a better situation.

If I tell you about all the shit I am going through and the bullshit I am dealing with, you will wonder how come I have not lost my mind or jumped off the bridge yet. I know we all are constantly worrying about something annoying or bugging the hell out of us. Or something more serious. But, I can only tell you from personal experience, that you are only causing yourself too much stress by constantly worrying about your problems or issues. I know it is not easy to come up with a solution, but if you spend more time trying to figure a way that will address your issues instead of just let them worry you, trust and believe, you will come up with ideas that might help deal better with the situation. Don't stress yourself. Everything will be ok if you try hard enough to make them ok. Please don't worry yourself to death.

When I was homeless, I woke up in my tent in the bushes under a tree one morning at sunrise and said to myself, here goes the sun rising. Which means that I woke up to see a new day. I am blessed and grateful to have been given the opportunity to be alive and see another day. How to make your day productive? If you are still alive, you are blessed. Don't worry about the little issues you have to face today. Just try your best and be happy you still here.

When I am stressed, I seek refuge in my mind, not to worry but to wonder. Spent time thinking about solutions and things you can or have to do to solve your issues.

Spending too much of your time worrying about your problems will only cause you stress and depression. Focus instead on how and what to do to solve them and you will be motivated.

Always remember that you are a wonderful and good human being. Don't get depressed over anyone not appreciating you and only trying to use you. The universe will deal with them. Take care of yourself and create peace within yourself. This message is for anybody who is stressed out by a relationship, in which they feel disrespected and taking advantage of when they give so much of themselves to help and please others. Please, don't allow others to depress you even though you feel hurt by their unkind behavior towards you. Keep your peace and take your time to figure the best way to handle the situation and come on top of it. Do not allow anyone to drive you crazy.

Don't let little things depress you. If you could only guess the hell that some of us are going through, you will understand that you have so much to be grateful for. Just take it easy on yourself.

My purpose is to motivate you and uplift you when you feel unhappy or stress. I want you to look at the shit I am going through and think of how fortunate you are for not having to go through this. And use that to appreciate the good things in your life instead of stressing other little things.

I was selling my book one day and started feeling stressed and anxious I had spent an hour or two without making a sale despite the hundreds of folks passing me by. I was not far from the entrance of the Old Ebbitt's Grill. A lot of rich folks and people who had money went in and out of there. I saw a limousine park behind me. The Driver came on the side and lifted his passenger on a wheelchair out of there. The man looked like he had a lot of money, but he was paralyzed entirely and could only move his hand from what I saw. I told myself, "wow, I am lucky to be able to walk and move around and be in relatively good health. I know this guy has a lot of money but I will rather be homeless and poor and in good health than have all the gold and diamond in the world and be paralyzed from head to toe."

If you are a little unhappy today because something is bothering you, I want to encourage you to focus on what to do to address what is bothering you and solve the issue.

I know how stress and depression and anxiety can suck the energy out of you and leave you in a state of confusion and mental anguish. So, if you are going through what I am talking about, know that I understand perfectly what you going through. Seriously, I feel you. I can't tell what I have been through in life. In my book, Homeless Lives Matter, Homeless My Story, I only talk maybe 10% of the hell I have been through. Even now, I am dealing with some issues and too scared to the doctor that whatever I am dealing with is cancer. But, I am dealing with whatever I got to deal with by being mentally and emotionally strong. Now, I was successful in getting out of the street. So at least I know I am not going to die on the streets in a tent or on somebody's couch, in case. So far, I am feeling great and healthy despite the sporadic pains in my back and else. I believe in miracles, but I believe that God is not going to come on earth to do things for us. He already created us with the tools to handle our business. It is up to us to do what we need to do to make things happen. Yes, we can pray for a miracle or wish ourselves good luck for situations beyond our control. But, we need to be mentally and emotionally strong to deal with life when we are dealing with stressful and depressing situations. That is how I feel about everything. But this is my opinion. To each his own.

But please appreciate the fact that you are still alive and given another opportunity to enjoy life. So, please there is so much to enjoy besides what is bothering you. I want to encourage you. There is always something good in your life to be happy about. Be happy. Look at me, I got all kinds of issues, but I am happy, I am still here and no longer homeless. In every situation, there is a solution. Just take your time and figure it out. Survival is a must. Don't stress.

When you feel stressed out for not being able to accomplish an immediate goal, just relax and observe nature around you. You will see a lot of interesting things going on around you. You will see a lot of natural and man-made beauty if you get off the mind of thinking of what is bothering you and concentrate on observing life around you.

One day I left my tent, walked my bike on the grass until I got to the sidewalk of the road. I got the only bike and starting pedaling until I noticed a plant growing the concrete-covered ground of the sidewalk. This is a lesson for all of us getting stressed over the adversities we are facing. Never give up, you can still make a way through, even in the most hostile environment.

I want to share with you some of the thought I shared daily on my Instagram page to encourage myself and my readers whenever I felt stressed, depressed or anxious about anything, while I was still homeless, hopefully, some of those thoughts inspire and motivate you because the whole purpose of this book is to inspire and motivate you:

-Sometimes, it feels like the more obstacles you remove out of your way, the more pile up and obstruct your path. Don't relent, keep trying even harder until things get better for you.

-Patience can be stressful. But please don't give in to desperation. When you know that you are putting the right efforts into the right actions and that you have realistic expectations, just be patient and keep doing the right thing. Don't give up trying. Leo

-Don't depress yourself over your problems, Focus more on how you can humble yourself and seek help and use the help to create opportunities for yourself to make things better.

-Spending too much of your time worrying about your problems will only cause you stress and depression. Focus instead on how and what to do to solve them and you will be motivated.

-Some of your folks don't want to see you happy. It seems like they love to see you going through hell and whatever they can do to make it worse for you, they will. Don't let it get to you. Be grateful to those who care about you.

-Sometimes strangers will show more compassion to you than your own relatives and close acquaintances, who will for no reason just act wicked towards you.

-I'd rather be a lonely poor homeless bum living in the woods in peace and harmony with nature and getting along with trees, birds, insects, than being around human beings who love drama and love being unhappy and miserable.

-I just believe that we should all be longing for peace and happiness. Otherwise, what is life worth if you have a good job, a roof over your head, a nice car, money in the bank, but want to be unhappy?

-I am not here to judge anybody, but it is obvious to me that some people just like to be miserable and make everybody around them miserable. I don't know what kind of gratification anyone will feel out of creating unhappiness inside their soul and around them.

-I cannot tell you how shameful and sad I have felt about my life as a homeless person. Even talking about it publicly is disgusting, to tell you the truth. I don't feel any pride coming up here and showing you another person's couch or living room where I sleep or kitchen where I cook my meal or a tent in the woods where I sleep. But, I can overcome those bad feelings and look at the greater picture, of how sharing my story can inspire and motivate so many of you and also create awareness about Homelessness and the reality of some of us who suffer from it.

-You will make mistakes and errors or face situations that will mess you up and cost you. Don't panic, don't be discouraged, and don't be angry at the whole world. Just pay the cost, learn from what went wrong and do better next time.

149

-Every homeless man or woman deserves a roof over their head whether or not they can afford it. No human being should be denied their human rights a house and even if they are poor and don't have enough money. I know the trauma and humanity of dwelling outside. I am still suffering from it.

-If you get stressed out very easily because of every hurdle on your path, you aren't going to get far or anywhere on your journey. Just relax, and figure out a way to go around, jump over and remove the hurdles from your path and keep moving forward. Don't allow stress and depression to slow you down or stop you.

-If you spend too much time staying depressed, happiness will remain an illusion. No matter what stresses you, try to make yourself happy under any circumstance. Always be aware that the time we had to live on this planet is very short.

-No matter how much pain and suffering you have been through and are still coming through, know that you deserve better and can get better. Never become too depressed. It will make you hopeless and make you make worse choices out of desperation. This is how I talk to myself. Sorry if I was too loud

-No matter what situation we find ourselves in, we have to either learn how to survive, or we will just allow difficulties to worsen our reality.

- When you feel stressed, angry, or depressed, find a way to de-stress and calm yourself down right away. Don't stay stressed and angry. And do not resort to alcohol and drug to do that. Not the solution.

-Use your mind to calm your mind down. You have the mental strength to mentally deal with stress and anger. If you don't, you will drive yourself insane.

-Don't make assumptions about people's reality based on what you see. You have no idea how much pain, suffering, and unhappiness they are silently going through.

- People can look happy but be going through a whole lot and not showing it.

-Everybody has some type of unhappy or stressful situation they dealing with that you might have no idea about. So try to understand people instead of judging them. Let's be compassionate and kind to one another.

-Don't worry about yourself too much when everything is not going your way. You are still alive, therefore able to try to make things a little better.

-Take it easy on your mind.

-Please, be happy or try to make yourself happy no matter what you are going through.

- Without happiness and peacefulness, life is not enjoyable no matter how much money and possession you have.

- Find something in your life to be happy about.

- I am walking by the cemetery to just reflect on life and my purpose in being here and whether I am using my time on this earth consciously, to make a positive contribution to humanity before my time is up and I am laid to rest in a place like this.

-Death is not what I am afraid of. I only hope that I can accomplish my purpose here before I make that transition and that when I am gone, humanity can remember me for something good. No matter what is going on in our life, we can still make a difference to make life better on Earth.

- I am admiring the beauty in my surroundings. Sometimes, the mind can be so consumed by worries that we pay little to no attention to the natural as well as man-created beauty in the surroundings that we are navigating through. Please, stop worrying too much about everything or little things. Just look around and you will see a lot of beautiful things to take your mind to another dimension where life can be contemplated for the beauty in it.

-One thing I have learned about stress is that it keeps you busy worrying. Worrying too much is exhausting, mentally and physically. If you are so *busy worrying, it will wear you out and make you feel unable to make moves because your energy will be so low. So please, take a break from worrying. Take actions to make things better, no matter what is distressing you. Leo*

-I went through so much hell for so long that I learned to keep my sanity by finding a way to create happiness within and sometimes around me.

- Those who followed my page since last spring can see how I made living in a tent under trees and in bushes, pleasant. So, I am not here to tell you to not be real with how you feel when the reality within and outside of you is painful and disturbing or just hard. All I am saying is that you still have to deal with it either by just allowing your predicament of undesirable circumstances to make you miserable and depressed or just sad, or just by enduring and find something to be happy about.

When you walk down the street feeling sad and worrying, please take your mind off your worries for just a minute and observe your surroundings. Lift your head up, and you might notice beautiful clouds. Or just pay attention to the buildings in your sight, and you may love their beautiful architectural designs. Or just observe the plants and trees or even the bugs and you will beauty and wonders around you.

-Life is happening around you whether you feel hopeless or not. So, be hopeful and try and try and try and try, and never despair or give up trying. There is always an end to a tunnel. Keep trying to get to it.

I-I am About to get up and start my day. Though I live outside, I am grateful to be able to wake up today and look at this beautiful nature around me and breathe the fresh and unpolluted air. I am grateful.

Everything is not that bad. We are surrounded by beauty from nature and also from human creativity and artistry.

There is so much to be grateful for no matter the predicament we in. Don't let stress suck the energy out of you. It is a beautiful day out there. Let me get up and take advantage of a bright sunny day.

It is raining outside. I am in here working on my next. Always occupy yourself constructively, even on a rainy day, whether you are homeless or you live a normal life. Don't make time for stress and depression to occupy your time.

Just woke up in my tent and observing the sun rising. Always a blessing to wake up to experience another day. When you wake up to see another day, don't stress about your problems. Instead, just be grateful and make the best of the day.

Despite the cloud in the path, the sun always shines. Leo Gnawa (Source Instagram/homelesslivesmatterbook)

Chapter 9

My last 10 months as a homeless

I want to share with you how I survived in my tent and on a friend's couch for the last year as a homeless until I finally and permanently ended my homelessness. These are quotes from posts that wrote almost daily on my Instagram page. I want you to inspire yourself and get motivated by my story so that you can also overcome whatever difficult situation you may be afflicted by. If you have an Instagram account, please go and follow me at homelesslesslivesmatterbook.com. Stay blessed. Leo

May 2020

-Coronavirus outbreak is making life harder for the homeless because everything is shut down. But in my tent, I use my imagination to create a meal that is healthy but cheap and easy to make.

-My meal of the day. Avocado mixed with Tuna in oil, mayo, ketchup, hot sauce. And organic fruit spread mixed with peanut butter. And Ritz crackers ha ha. I am surviving the best I can in isolation.

-The Laundromat where I normally wash my clothes, has been shut down since the Coronavirus outbreak.

- I figured out that, I could spread my larger tarp on the grass and capture some rainwater last week when it rained for a couple of days. Then use the rainwater to wash my clothes and dry them the next day when it was sunny.

155

-Even the dirtiest thing can be cleaned up just like our body, mind, and spirit. I cleaned that dirty nasty chair I got out of the trash last night. I used gain detergent I had for laundry.

-The other day, two security officers came and told me that I could not be here. But hey, I am back again. I got to write. Public libraries are closed, because of covid 19. But I still got to write my next book. The hell with covid 19. It ain't gonna stop me from writing wherever I can find a place to keep my laptop charged.

I am feeling a little stressed. It is 7:24 pm. This is my meal for the entire day. Just two cans of tuna with mayo and some herbs and spices seasonings and some strawberry fruit spread on the side. And some mountain dew. I normally don't consume that much soda drink, but once in the blue moon. I am here in the woods, trying to survive the best I can until this Coronavirus nonsense go away and everything gets back to normal.

-I am watching these pigeons as I am feeding them and am saddened by the selfishness and greed some of them exhibit. I would think these traits were invented by human beings. It was enough food for all of them. At least we humans have a higher consciousness and should not act like these animals. We should learn how to share. This planet can produce enough food for every single human being. Let us be altruistic and let us share.

-My meal of the day. Tuna and mayo with some spices and crackers again. Yes, it is depressing to eat the same thing over and over and over again every day. But hey, it is healthy and I will not starve during this pandemic shut down. I can survive on the tuna and crackers u till things get back to normal. I stay right here away from everybody, so I won't worry about catching Coronavirus. I can't afford to get sick. So I am here in the woods (not totally) and surviving on the little food I got here. I am grateful.

-I am updating my website right now, outside here while charging my laptop. The security guards of the building ask me to leave several times in the past. But when you homeless and have no home you charge your stuff, hey they chase you, but you don't give up. Hope one day, I won't have to go through so much suffering and humiliation. But hey, that's life. I am grateful.

-I have been outside here for 7 hours working on my website while charging my phone outside here and using WIFI. A security guard did his round a couple of times and did not bother me. Lucky me

-Just took a hot shower at the Downtown Day Services Center for the homeless, located inside the New York Ave. Presbyterian Church at 1313 New York Ave. NW. I had to make a reservation on Tuesday to be able to take a shower today. I am glad they are still doing showers although on appointment even though they are not providing all the services as usual and only allowing inside the building, whoever has an appointment for shower or laundry.

-The days I got to wait till I can make it to a hot shower, I just go get a gallon or two of water at a corner store about 7 blocks down the street and shower right outside my tent. I don't care how cold the weather and the water are, I got to shower every day. Being homeless doesn't mean that you got to forget about your hygiene. No excuse not to clean your body every day. Sorry. I got to.

-Hey, I also had to wash my clothes. The Laundromat where I normally do my laundry is not open back yet cause of Coronavirus restrictions. Cause I am homeless doesn't mean I got to feel comfortable wearing dirty clothes. It is always a way, no matter what. We always got to try to find a solution to any issue we face. If I am not giving up. You shouldn't. Stay blessed, whoever you are.

-I stashed my little bucket, body wash, and lotion in these bushes. Wow, they are still there. About to take a quick shower outside here while the streets are still deserted. I had to ride 20 some minutes down here to be able to shower outside here before I start my day. Need to be fresh to start a new day with a clear mind. No matter what you go through, stop complaining. No need to depress yourself. Just do what you got to do to feel better.

-Blake and Sarah, two strangers I met on Instagram, cared enough to bring me 17 gallons of water and some packs of Tuna and crackers. I don't know how to thank them enough for taking their precious time and drive all the way up here to give water to a 55-year-old homeless man living in the bushes. I am so touched; I don't know what to say.

JUNE 2020

-I just got home. It is 12:10 am. Yes, pitch dark. But my eyes see pretty good in the dark. Sometimes I feel like a wild animal. But we are party animals and we can use the animal part of us not to harm other humans but to survive under harsh circumstances. Darkness may be scary, but I think darkness is also beautiful and very peaceful. Good night.

-Just caught a march. I wish I could join. I am so proud of these kids protesting under the rain. Thank you so much to each and everyone who spoke out against police brutality and senseless killings of black folks. Special thanks to all these white kids standing up and racism. People of the world, we are one.

-9:45pm. I just rode and passed the Safeway store. Seeing this old man going to sleep right outside on the sidewalk while it is still drizzling. It just rained. Pavement still wet. That makes me so sad. I don't know what to say.

-I got soaked last night on my way back. Once here, I spread a tarp and captured rainwater. I am filtering it in a 3-gallon bottle and will add a bit of alcohol to disinfect and use it to clean up. I saved the rest for the future so I won't use my drinking water for hygienic purposes. Always try to make the best of the situation even on a rainy day. Rainwater, free water. Use it.

-I am riding my bike to rally at the White House. Crossing. in Franklyn Park, NW Washington DC. Homeless tents everywhere. There is a Homelessness epidemic. It is not getting better. America wakes up.

-I walk barefoot sometimes to keep my feet connected to the earth and its natural vibration. Wearing shoes and socks 90% of the time and walking on concrete 24/7 disconnect us from the earth and reduce our instincts, I think. So occasionally, I just walk on the earth and the natural elements to connect with mother earth.

-I am watering my tomato plants with rainwater I captured and save a couple of days ago. Even a homeless person can grow food. All you need is a slice of tomato with grains in it and some soil. Water is free from the rain. Just figure a way to capture when it rains and save it in empty water bottles. Where there is a will there away.

-We are still in phase 1 opening here in DC (Coronavirus pandemic restrictions). If you have washing and drying machines in your house or your building, consider yourself blessed. It is people outside here who have to go through headaches to get their clothes washed. So enjoy your blessings and don't complain about insignificant things. Somebody out here is doing worse than you. Don't worry. Be happy.

-This raven showed up this morning on the tree branches atop of my tent and starting making loud annoying noises. Luckily I had some bread. The rest is in this video. I am sharing this habitat with these living beings. They know I got some food, so they come here expecting me to share with them. If I can, I do without hesitation. We all got to eat.

-I went and got myself 7 T-shirts for $10 at Forman Mills. Have to go to the laundromat tomorrow to wash my clothes. It is open back now. Thank you to those who have ordered my book or sent in donations. This is how I am using the money from my selling my books or getting donations.

Wow, my tomatoes are growing. I planted them around my tent. I wanted them to grow straight from the ground. This is just an experiment full of symbolism for me. No matter what predicament or misfortune we find ourselves in, we need to plant the seed of hope and actions to grow out of it.

-I Spread a tarp on the ground to collect rainwater to use to shower. Homeless or not, no excuse, I still got to wash my behind. Free water from the sky. For every situation, there is a solution. Just take your time and figure it out. Survival is a must. Don't stress.

-I am riding my bike by this woman sleeping under scaffolds by an apartment housing construction side at 3:00 pm under 83-degree temperature.

-Laundromat closed earlier. Couldn't make it. Had to hand wash few clothes items to have some clean to wear till I get to laundry tomorrow. As I always remind all of you, there is always some kind of solution to a difficult situation. So don't let any problem stress you. Yes, I am in downtown Washington dc handwashing my clothes. So what if somebody sees me? Can't let pride and shame get in the way.

-I stashed a laundry bag filled with dirty clothes and a bottle of Gain detergent in these bushes here in downtown Washington DC, till tomorrow when I am finally able to get to the laundromat up the street. I am not worried about anybody stealing dirty clothes. If they do, then they must really need it. I won't be mad. I have received donations via Paypal a couple of days ago.

July 2020

-I Just took a nice shower outside my tent. Feeling fresh. About to go downtown ship few more books and take care of business. Forget my issues, worries, or problems. I got to stay focused on turning this day into a productive day, by the time I get back here late in the night. If you have not ordered your book yet, what you waiting on? Come on, we all got to eat! Haha. Stay blessed.

-I just stopped at Walmart to get some new flip-flops for $9.99, cause the ones I am wearing now are worn out. When I used to sell my books on the streets, some of the folks come and chat with me, would ask me if it was a good thing to give money to homeless beggars. My thing is this, it is not all homeless folks who will use your money for alcohol or drugs. Some of the homeless out there may need to replace their shoes very bad or some homeless women may need some intimate toiletries urgently. So you never know what a homeless will do with money. I am not telling you what to do. I am just showing you through my experience what homeless folks can do with money.

-Earlier today. Warplanes flying over the city here in Washington DC on today's 4th of July. I am totally against the war, but I like to see planes fly into the sky just because I admire human creativity and ingenuity. I wish these planes could be used only for peaceful purposes. Let us create a culture of peace and tolerance so that these planes can only be used for deterrence and mostly for entertainment like today and not for inflicting destruction on humanity and mother nature.

-I didn't realize that this plant around my tent was poison ivy until my skin started itching very badly and bumps appearing all over the infected areas. I was gardening and inadvertently came in contact with the poisonous leaves. Now I am trying to figure a way to get rid of them at least in my immediate surrounding. I heard that spraying them with vinegar and water kills them fast. Well, I guess the lesson today is this. A little caution will preserve you from some unwanted afflictions.

-Back to my spot. About to set up my new tent. I spent a day indoors and feel rejuvenated although it was hot in my friend's apartment and AC was barely working. It feels better out there. Breeze and fresh air although it feels like 90 degrees out here. Sometimes people wonder why the homeless prefer to stay outside rather than go to a shelter or at a friend's house. There are reasons why. Homeless folks will stay wherever they feel comfortable even though it may not be the most desirable habitat.

-I came to my friend's apartment for a night. I give him $20 for a night whenever I decide to come here to feel in a cool place and escape the heat. my tent.

-I am turning from L St North East to North Capitol Street. There are more homeless sleeping in tents by the building. As I said, if you are in Washington DC, it's gonna be above 100 degrees today. You can bring these folks some cold water if you feel like doing some charity today. Put the water bottles in your freezer so they will be frozen when you come out. It will surely melt by the time you get to them. But it will still be very cold and they will enjoy it.

-I want to express my gratitude to Laney for dropping a cooler, some ice, and some water by my tent a few minutes ago. Thank you so much to all of you who take some of your time to show compassion for the homeless. Thank you again, Laney (laneybogs08). Stay blessed

-When I used to sell books on the street before the Coronavirus pandemic shut everything down, some skeptical folks who stopped to check my book, used to ask me, how could I be a homeless person living on the street and write a book? I never understood why people feel like homelessness is an impairment. Nothing is impossible. I am writing my next book now regardless of the high temperature. I wrote my previous book when it was cold and my fingers were so cold, I had to stop and rub them together. I just hope this book comes out as great work. But, I am not letting the heat stop me. I am glad it is cooling off a little bit. They call for a thunderstorm but I have not seen a drop of rain yet. Don't let rain, cold, heat, or anything stop or prevent you from doing what you got to do to accomplish an important goal.

-I try to stay positive but sometimes situations can be overwhelming, but I am still ok. First, I just left the clinic to get checked for a lump in my chest above my heart, that has been bothering me for a week now. The doctor thinks it might be fibrosis. But she gave me a referral to get a mammogram. Hopefully, it is not cancer. When I stepped outside, my bike tire was gone. Somebody stole my bike wheel while my bike was locked right in front of the clinic. The security dude let me keep the bike inside the facility till tomorrow at 9:00 am cause I cannot carry the bike on the bus without the back tire. This was not a good day. But I am not gonna complain. Haha. Left laughed before I get too upset and shed tears. Can't afford to do that. Being 54 years old and going through so much hardship is not nice haha. But I am still alive. Something to be grateful for I guess. Although it is a f-cked up life. I guess it is just bad luck. I will be ok.

-I am finally back to the place I call home. I apologize for having been weak earlier. I am trying to uplift and inspire many of you to be strong in the face of adversities. So I am to be my best student. But it is ok to be upset and let one true feeling out when under stress. But we have to pick ourselves back up and not stay in a stressful mood. So, I am gonna take a nap and enjoy the calm presence of nature around me.

-Now who am I to blame? I left my tent this morning without covering it. Just got a severe flash flooding warning alert on my phone for this area till 6:30 pm. I am stuck here in the back alley loading dock where I was charging my phone and laptop and making phone calls for medical appointments. By the time I am thinking about getting my stuff together and put the bike on the bus and head to the tent to cover it, here comes thunderstorms and heavy rain. I know my bed is soaked wet. Haha. But it is my fault. I should have checked the weather forecast this morning before rushing to the clinic to get my bike. One problem solved, another created. So goes life. Anyway, it has been hot and will remain hot. It may feel nice to sleep in a wet bed outside haha. Hey, I am not complaining. I am alive can't complain. Just sharing with you what the homeless go through every day. And my case is not even worse than many out there who have no tent and sleep on the concrete. I have shared pics of some of them with you. I am just happy for my plants (tomatoes and garlic). They needed the rain.

-Before I left this morning, I opened the tent wide to let everything dry. I am back before the rain forecast for 7:00 pm, starts. I made sure I checked the weather this morning and got back here in time. When I got back here last night after the storm, the floor of my tent was flooded. I emptied the water in a bucket and will use it to water my tomato plants. Surprisingly, my tent-top mattress was not soaked. I had a peaceful sleep.

-When I came back the night before Yesterday, my tent was flooded. I did not look at the water on my tent floor as a problem. I collected it and fill a 7-gallon water jar plus another water gallon bottle and save all that water for my tomato and garlic plants. It had been really hot lately and the plants were dying until the storm breaks these last two days. But the heat may resume soon and at least I got water saved for the plant. Water may look dirty because dirt may have got in, but the plants will benefit from it. A lesson of the day, turn a problem into a solution, maybe not for you but someone else or an element of nature.

-Came to my buddy's place to take a long cold shower. On my way back to my tent before rain starts. Finding a place to take a shower can be a headache for the homeless, mostly for women out there.

163

-I would like to ask any of you who have any kind of connection with the folks who run the place called SOME, which has a daily shower service for homeless men and women, to try themselves to take a shower there and tell you if it is ok to have three showers that only run burning hot water with low pressure to the point where not only you risk burning your skin taking a shower there, but there is barely enough water running out of the 3 showers. It is simply ridiculous that it has been like that for almost a year and no one cares to fix it. I had stopped going there since the pandemic but tried over the day and nothing changed. But there are homeless men and women so desperate for a shower who still go there morning to hot an extremely hot shower under this heatwave. Makes no sense.

-Got my tent covered this time. Rain started. The lesson of the day. Always be prepared mostly for predictable situations. If you don't then the calamity that comes your way will be self-inflicted. Learn that lesson from the last time when I did not check the weather forecast and left without covering my tent and came back to find the tent flooded.

August 2020

-It is 5:30 am. I feel very hungry. Just got some mocha, a can of tuna salad snack, and two bananas from 7/11. I woke up around 3:30 am to some noise outside my tent. When I peeped through the screen I saw some pair of eyes shining in the dark outside towards me. I thought of either a cat or a raccoon. Most probably a raccoon. Anyway, when you sleep outside, you are subjected to be awakened constantly by all sorts of noises and the abrupt presence of animals or humans in your immediate surrounding.

-I was blessed by Yoojin and her friends. They just brought me a small table and a chair. Now I can write in my tent. I broke the chair I had and with no table and chairs, it is very hard to write inside a tent. I want to express my gratitude to Yoojin and her friends. Thank you so much

-It rained abundantly the previous couple of days. As some of you already know, I do collect rainwater as I am doing this morning, and filter it and use it for personal hygiene or to water the tomatoes and garlic I am growing

164

around here. I am not drinking it though. I could not make it to a shower place, so I have to shower out there. I wear long short that reaches my knees, so I won't be accused of indecent exposure although no pedestrians are walking by and the cars on the road cannot see me because I am behind my tent. There is no human habitat or business around here. It is only nature and peace and quietness. So I am not bothering anybody, as we say in the street language.

-Wow, look at this thing, whatever you call it, crawling on my tent. I normally don't kill these little creatures as long as they don't try to bite me or mess with me. I am in their natural habitat, so I can see them as invaders of my space. If anything it is quite the opposite. Even when I see spiders in my tent, I just move them out. I don't hurt them. Now mosquitoes? Haha. I try to fan them out of the tent with some clothes but when they sit on my skin and try to suck the blood out of me? Nope. They might get hurt. I feel sorry even when I have to slap them and kill them by accident hahaha. I So I am not bothering this little crawling thing on top of my tent, although it senses danger and is moving faster. Lil thing, you're alright. Leo is not gonna bother you. Sometimes we just hurt these little creatures only because we don't like what they look like, although they are harmless. But we got to understand that value their life as much as we value ours. So please don't kill them. If you don't want them in your space or face, at least remove them without hurting them. We can learn so much from them. Remember that whoever created them also created us. We all are here on this planet earth for a purpose. Let focus on finding and executing ours and let others live to accomplish what they are here for.

-I am about to go to sleep on somebody's couch tonight with a fan blowing right above my head in this old building with a ceiling fan barely blowing some air and with no air conditioner. Though I prefer my bed in my tent to a couch, I am still grateful that my friend opens his doors to me to come inside anytime I feel the need to come inside. At least I can sleep tonight without hearing insects and birds making all sorts of noises all night, haha. Anyway. Hopefully, I wake up in the morning to see another day.

- Just waking up on somebody's couch. Kind of missing my bed in my tent. Sleeping on a couch gives me neck pains that I don't need now. Haha. But I am grateful that somebody opened their door to me for a night and in exchange, I could also help them with $20 that they can use since they are also poor.

-8:00 am. Riding my bike by this homeless man sleeping in the median lane during heavy morning traffic on one of Washington DC's busiest highways. Seems like homelessness is getting worse. Anybody paying attention?

-9:45pm. I had gone to my tent, a couple of hours ago. But because of the rain these couple of days, it seems like the whole area around my tent is infested with mosquitoes. It was a little stressful to have to deal with the humidity and mosquitoes. So I called my friend and asked if I could come and sleep on his couch for tonight. He said yes. I made a stop at the Giant store and got myself some stuff to cook while I am here for the night. I got dishwashing soap since I know he had a little bottle the last time I was here and most likely he had run out. I gave him $20 as usual for a night.

-4:13 pm. I am walking by a cemetery and feeling like it is the place to rest in peace after suffering so much in this life. But no rush, hahaha. We all gonna end up there. Until then, I can only try to feel ok even when feeling depressed.

10:08 pm. I just returned to my friend's place from my tent. I just warmed up the food I cooked last night. This is why I came back here, haha. I went back to my tent this morning around 11 am and did some clean-up. Then went down the street to get some bag of ice. I came back around 1 pm and once I got on my bed in my tent, I fell into a deep sleep. Got awakened by the rain and got back to sleep till 7 pm. Although it is pleasant to come to my buddy's place and sleep on his couch, I don't get real sleep because a couch is not as comfortable as sleeping in my bed in my tent.

-7:00pm. I just woke up in my tent after taking a nap when I came back from returning to my friend's place to pick up my solar charger that I forgot when I had come to my tent the first time this afternoon. When I return here and rest on my bed, I fell into a deeper and restful sleep than sleeping on a couch. Many homeless do not get appropriate sleep because they

166

don't sleep on a comfortable bed. So one thing I made sure of, is to have brought a bed here in my tent. Although it is better to be indoors than outside, at least I got this bed here which makes sleeping out here more restful.

-10:10am. Left my tent at 8:00 am. Got to SOME and took a shower by 8:45 am. Now I am having breakfast (and most likely my only meal of the day) outside on a bench. Having fried croaker fish with fried eggs and home fries and bread a grape jelly and Ice tea lemonade mix. All for $10.20 from carry-out on New York and New Jersey Ave. in North West DC. My book is my source of income. It allows me to eat what I want.

-2:53pm. Sitting at a bus stop in downtown DC a little disoriented but I am ok. About to jump on my bike and head back to my tent. Was here for an appointment for an emergency. But it got rescheduled. I guess patience instead of sadness is how you deal with such a situation.

 -9:15 am. Another frustrating start today. I left SOME at around 8:50 am. I went there to take a shower. I left my tent at 8:20 am. I got to SOME at 8:32 am. I was the only one standing outside at the door for a shower. On the door, the sign says "Men showers from 6:00 am to 9:30 am and women Showers from 9:45 to 11:30 am.

-I decided to let the gentleman doing the showers know that I was waiting. I opened the door and saw him talking in the dining room with other workers. I waited till he stepped out of the dining room and told him that I was waiting to take shower. He told me that the two homeless in showers were the last ones for the day. I closed the door and asked a lady outside what time it was. She told me 8:42 am. I opened the door back and asked another worker to call the supervisor for me. The gentleman steps back from the showers area as the lady supervisor walked towards the door. The gentleman stood right behind her. I asked to talk to her alone. He responded, "you gonna talk about me, so I want to hear". I asked to talk to her in private. She asked me to meet her in front of the building. I did but she never came. I returned to the entrance door. The gentleman stood there. I told him, I just want to make suggestions to her for some changes in the way this shower thing is run because it is so frustrating to come there at 8:38 am and be told that the shower is done for the day when the sign says showers end at 9:30 am. Then he changed the story. "you came here at 8:45 am and I told you that you might not be able to make it to the showers", he said. I told him that I talked to him at 8:38 am and he told me showers closed for the day after those in there come out. I got on my bike and left.

-The real issue here is that the gentleman is lazy and doesn't care about the homeless waiting to take shower. He normally sits at his desk and spends the entire time on his cellphone instead of monitoring the time each person spent in the shower so that the next person waiting can get in. Then he rushes to close the shower early. And he never clean showers after last used, for the next person. Things like that frustrate and discourage many homeless for taking showers at places offering service to the homeless.

-8:26 pm. I walked by this barefoot homeless woman sleeping on a street corner in Washington DC, as I am about to cross the street to the bus stop. The plight of homeless women makes me so sad. How is this possible in the downtown area of the capital city of the wealthiest and most powerful nation on planet earth?

-4:22pm. Sitting in the park feeding birds and also getting clothes I stashed in the bushes here to hand wash some until I can get the rest to the laundromat tomorrow. Will be heading to my tent tonight after spending few nights at a friend's place. I need to get to my tent before it starts raining tonight.

-1:30pm. I am back in my tent from downtown. About to eat this meal that this lady cooked for me. Every Sunday she fixes me a meal and I go pick it up by the senior citizen building where she leaves. She is one of my angels. At least I know, every Sunday someone cares to make sure I got a home-cooked meal.

- I did not sleep so well last night. My tent was wet and mosquitoes had got in when I tried to get water out the previous night when I return from staying indoors. Additional rain all day yesterday kept everything wet outside. Now it is sunny and beautiful. I removed to cover off the tent and I am about to try to get some sleep after I need. It is nice and breezy and sunny. Feels nice under the trees.

-18:40am. I Just finished taking shower at SOME and am about to get on my bike to my next destination (laundromat). The guy who regularly does the shower is off today. What a relief! Today, the old man who had been running the showers for a long time but has been moved to the dining area is filling in for the guy in charge of showers now. I told the old man that he is so much because he uses to do a very good job, making sure everybody gets in the shower. But the one there now is doing a terrible job. Somebody else told me the other day, that he had come at 7:40 am and waited for the shower. But at 8:15 am, the shower guy told him that it was taking any more people and that was it for the day. The signs say "men showers

--6:00am to 9:30am. This is what the homeless go through. Nobody checks how the services are rendered and the homeless are too afraid to complain because they still have to come back and deal with the same folks. Sad but the truth.

-1:15 am. I caught a flat tire. I stopped at a store to get inner tubes but they don' t have 27" tubes. So I bought a patch kit and am heading to my friend's house so he can fix it for me. I am far from my tent and closer to his place. I don't have any tools on me. It is drizzling. I don't know if I will be able to accomplish everything I planned for the day.

September 2020

-2:30pm. I am getting my dirty clothes stashed in some bushes to take them to the laundry.

-10:40pm. Finally got to my friend's place after a stop at a Giant Store to pick me some fresh vegetables and fish. Now I am in my friend's kitchen fixing myself a meal after I took a nice shower though I took one earlier at some. Sorry, mosquitoes and insects, and birds, I am not keeping you company tonight. It is good for a homeless person to be able to go indoors from time to time and feel like a human beings instead of a wild animal.

-6:35 pm. I Just got to my tent. I am being attacked by millions of Mosquitos. It rained for the last couple of days that I was away. And I am being bitten left to right. They just invaded the whole area cause it is still wet. I think I am going back to my friend's place in North East.

- 9:30pm. I returned indoors for a couple of nights in somebody's living room and couch. It feels so relaxing to be indoors compared to sleeping outside. It is so stressful to be homeless sleeping outside. Every homeless had a chance to go inside somewhere calm and relaxing where they can spend a few nights of the week, inside. Living outside is very depressing. You got to be mentally strong to sleep outside every night. I am grateful for a night indoors.

-10:50am . This morning, I passed this mattress with a " PRIVATE PROPERTY" notice on it. It was left by a homeless person under the bridge on K St between 1st and 2nd Street, NE. The purpose of the notice is to prevent cleaning crews from trashing his bed. All tents have been removed from under the bridge on K street between 1st and 2nd street. But they are allowed so far under the same bridge on L and M street, North East, Washington DC.

-7:15 pm. On the train to the computer store in Rockville Maryland. Just arrived at my destination at Twinbrook station. Never been to this store. But supposed to be around the corner from the station. I need this computer fixed. Need you to order books so I can earn enough money to cover for the cost of repair.

-8:15pm. I came by Safeway to meet albaptist08 who brought me some comforter and pillows after I posted earlier about going to Forman Mills to get some blanket. Now, I don't need to worry about purchasing a blanket. It is a bit chilly outside here and I am getting on the bus to head to my tent.

Thank you so much to Alex and all the angels out here who care for the homeless.

-10:20pm. I am in some downtown Washington DC back alley loading dock, charging my phone before heading to my tent for the night. Another homeless man sleeping in the doorway.

-11:00am. I am just waking up and about to take a cold shower outside my tent. It was chilly throughout the night. The cover I received from albaptiste08 kept me warm. Thank you again, Alex. You are an angel.

-4:46 pm. I am checking on some of the tomatoes I planted a few months ago around me as an experiment when the coronavirus epidemic started and everything got shut down. I had planned to grow food in the woods in case things had got worse and food scarce. When toilet paper, then water, then bread shelves started getting empty as stores, O had to think of plan B in case the shortages had extended to major food items and everybody started looking for food. Haha. Homelessness has tough me a lot about survival. You got to think ahead instead of panicking when uncertainty shows on the horizon. That is one of the things I am writing about in my next book.

-9:21 AM. I am waking up in my tent. Too late now to shower at SOME. Men shower there is from 6:00 am to 9:00 am. So they say. But if you don't make it there by 8:00 am, chances are, you won't get in showers. Women showers time is from 9:45 am to 11:00 am in the same showers after the men. So I am gonna have to bathe outside my tent. This is one advantage of setting my tent in nature and seclusion. The birds and trees and bushes will not accuse me of indecent exposure.

-My back tire exploded while I was riding my bike a few nights ago. I am about to use some of the money I have raised so far to go buy a new wheel and a new tire and a new inner tube. My bike is my most reliable means of transportation.

- 2:16 PM. I just woke up off somebody's couch and am anxiously waiting for the UPS man to deliver the box of books I ordered over 2 weeks ago from the manufacturer.

171

-7:30 pm. I am still at the window waiting for the UPS man to deliver the book shipment I have been waiting sitting at the window all day. In this type of neighborhood, you can't take a chance with a package sitting on the porch. As I sat there, I just witness police on foot chasing and arresting a juvenile. They thought they have lost him for a minute when they got to the fenced dead end of a one-way street. But the boy was hiding in a bush by the building next to my friend's. I am it ended with a peaceful arrest although I was a bit concerned when one officer run across the street with her drawn when another officer spotted the young man hidden in the bushes. I know there have been so many incidents with police shooting black folks. But there are a lot of good cops out who are doing their job professionally.

-7:40pm. I spot a UPS truck pulling up the street and parking in front of my friend's building. I let my friend know since I ordered the books to his name because they are delivered to his address. I wish they could deliver them to my tent. Just joking. Hahaha. He picked it up for me. I got to wait till the morning to ship most of the book orders. I two more shipments on the way. It cost me money to order the books.

October 2020

-4:30 pm. Another Angel, by the name of Faith, finds a bike for me from her circle of bike riders. She asked around if someone had a free bike, and here we. She drove her hour away to bring me this bike. I am so amazed and humbled by the kindness and support I am getting from many of you reading my posts here. Thank you a lot Faith for this bike. It will help a great deal during this period of the coronavirus pandemic. At least I don't have to worry about public transportation. A bike will take me anywhere. I am grateful.

-12:06 PM. After sleeping on someone's couch for a week in order so that I could be indoors, away from mosquitoes, I am finally back in my bed. But my bed outside, in a tent of course. More comfortable than a couch though.

. But sleeping on somebody's couch inside a house, is preferable to doing so on a comfortable bed outside. I am not trying to glamorize the homeless by any means. But, I can sleep see something enjoyable in every situation, good or bad. So I am gonna enjoy this bed and not the fact that it bothers me because it is outside. I am grateful.

I am Charging my portable power with my solar charger right by the tent in nature. One of the Angels who have supported and helping for a long time, got it for me when the pandemic started so that I could be safe and not worry about coming downtown to charge my phone. I receive so many blessings from total strangers and I am grateful for that. I also feel it as a duty to use the extra I get to help also those around me in dire need, whenever I can.

-Me fooling around with this praying mantis climbing on my bike. I just love observing these beautiful little creatures in this natural environment, which they don't mind sharing with a homeless man. We need to stop destroying the environment so that is their natural habitat, otherwise, these beautiful creatures will become extinct.

-9:30 am. I am Walking barefoot to be in touch with nature and get the energy directly from mother nature with concrete or asphalt in between. Being in touch with nature, breathing fresh air, listening to birds and insects, and just looking at the greenery in my surround soothes my soul and relaxes my mind. I advise everybody to sometimes take a walk in a natural environment and connect with nature. It's healing. Anyway, I need a shower haha. So I am going to somebody's place to take a shower. It is a little chilly outside here. Normally. I would just shower outside my tent. But I feel like going indoors to shower. I have raised enough money.

- I want to congratulate Jessica Kuhn Boisseau (jessbsellsthedmv) and thank her from the deepest of my soul for having successfully completed a Gofundme campaign she started on Sept 1, 2020, to raise $1500 to offer me a new laptop and help me with the rest of the funds. Although she successfully raised $1889 in only 3 days, she had to patiently wait until this morning to finally receive the money in the amount on the picture. I know it was agonizing for her to wait for over a month to receive the funds that were supposed to be sent by the fifth day from the time she requested it.

-Haha. Sometimes, I feel safer around animals, wildlife, and trees, and plants. Human beings are the most dangerous creatures on this planet. This is why we all need to contribute to increasing compassion, empathy, and respect for our fellow humans.

-7.00pm. I just purchased a new computer for $741 and a phone for $220 with the GoFundMe money raised by Jessica and also the fundraiser I did here on Instagram a couple of weeks ago The campaign was initiated to get me a new computer so I can resume writing and finished my second. I was very upset when I got here because I waited for a month and they never called me about the laptop I I left here for repair. And now they are telling me that there is a problem with the motherboard, and repair gonna cost me $500. This is ridiculous. Thank you to everybody who donated and special thanks to Jessica Boisseau for. this computer. I am grateful.

-12:00pm. I finally set up a new laptop. I downloaded Microsoft office for $145. So the laptop is good to go. I can resume writing my next book now and work on my website again. My other laptop is still at Microcenter. I am not paying $500 for repair. This is crazy. So, I want to think of Jessica Boisseau (jessbsellsthedmv) and everybody who donated for me to get this laptop. As a self-published homeless activist-author, this laptop was much needed to finish my next book

-To Faith (1faithamber). I want to thank you so much for this bike you got from friends and brought to me by driving all the way for an hour from Maryland. I really have not had a road bike in God knows how long. But this is a perfect means of transportation for a homeless man like me living in a remote place. This bike is so great. Many of you who have purchased and read my book, have reached back and told me that if I needed anything to just let you know. But most of the time, I just say, I am ok, I appreciate you but I don't need anything now. But if I urgently need anything like I needed a bike and a laptop or a chair or folding table or a blanket and somebody is offering me one, I can only consider myself fortunate and blessed that someone is willing to donate these items to me or even some money for me to get them.

November 2020

-4:45pm. I just met Alexandra and her friend Patrick. She purchased two copies of my book. I wanted to offer them as a gift but she wanted to pay for them. Both of them had venmoed me some donation in the past towards getting shipping supplies for shipping my books. They also brought some stuff that I can use at my tent. I am very grateful for many of you who have extended so much humanity and kindness to me. I am thankful. Thank you, Alexandria. Thank you. Patrick.

-12:00am. Stopping by the cemetery on my way back to my friend's place. I believe that I am on this earth for a purpose and that I am not gonna be here forever. So stopping by a graveyard helps me appreciate life even in the predicament I am and understand that time is pretty short.

-I am here with the crowd at the White House today Saturday, November 7, 2020, witnessing history taking its course. The first woman elected Vice-president of the United States. I also came across this homeless brother. Not a Trump supporter. I don't agree with his choice of some of the words he used to refer to Trump. But those words are street vernacular. But today, after a long depressing wait, a winner was declared by the media. some are happy, others are not. This is Democracy. Somebody wins, somebody loses. But life goes on. We still got to love one another.

-This young lady has been a real Angel to me. She is one of the first people who ordered a copy of my book since I started this Instagram page a few months. And since she read my book she has been sending me donations from the sales of some of her handmade jewelry. I am so grateful to her. She is an Angel. Sometimes, I am not comfortable asking people to donate. I prefer that people just purchase my book so I feel like I am earning every penny I am making. But I am humble enough to accept donations because I am not selling enough books online as I normally was when I was selling my books on the street before the coronavirus pandemic. Bel Hammond

175

has been donating from selling her jewelry, many times when I was not getting book orders. I am trying to figure how to one day create the opportunity to express my gratitude to everybody who supported my book and donated. And especially those who donate a lot. I am so grateful to bel and her mother who also has supported my book and donated more than once. I appreciate all of you who have supported my book. Stay blessed. L

-Election is over, homelessness is not. No matter who won, not much going to change. One side happy, another sad. In reality, nobody wins when suffering is still around. I normally do not involve my, religious and ideological opinions when I am creating awareness about homelessness and sharing my story. I am sure on both sides, there are genuinely compassionate good souls out there caring about the homeless. So I am careful not to offend anyone by voicing any personal opinion. When I used to sell my books outside on 15th and G, a block away from the White House, I had folks from all religious and ideological persuasions walking by and checking on my book. I, therefore, had to be careful when talking to people so that I won't offend them. One day, there were two big protests a day apart from each other here in Washington DC. One was a Women March against Trump attracting a more liberal crowd, and the other,

-5:50pm. I got the tent set back up. I didn't nail it to the ground very tight the last time I left. I will be back tomorrow morning to take everything out and mostly the mattresses and let them dry all day. I might have to spend tomorrow night on my friend's couch because I need to let the inside of the tent dry out. Some rain got into it. But that's my fault. I didn't plan to be gone for so long

-I am waiting for the bus because I know it will get here. Patience can be excruciating, but it is not in vain when you know what you are patient about will be fulfilled. Be patient, don't give up. 10:40pm. I am here at the bus stop with my bike and a load of mailing supplies on my bike. A little frigid out here. I have a long way to go. But I don't feel like riding my bike. So I got to wait for the bus. It means I got to wait because I know the bus will here.

176

-I came to pick my Thanksgiving dinner from Yesterday. This will also be my birthday dinner. This nice lady that I have known from her from Franklin Park in NW Washington DC, where they use to feed and hand out hygiene stuff and clothes the Homeless. Her name is Arlene. When the Coronavirus pandemic shut everything down, I could no longer make money selling copies of my book, Homeless Lives Matter, Homeless My Story, on the street. Though I had lost touch with her, she reached to me to check on me and offered to cook a homemade meal for me every Sunday. The last Sunday, I met her, she told me she was gonna have a Thanksgiving dinner for me. When she called Yesterday, I slept in the day after I spent nearly 24 sleepless hours getting book orders ready. So I did not have Thanksgiving dinner Yesterday. I am about to enjoy this meal prepared by this angel. I feel so blessed to have all these angels around me. I believe that angels are a real human being that shows up on your path at the right time to bless you unexpectedly. I am so great that despite all the miserable experiences I have been having, there are still great human beings out there who can empathize without casting judgment.

-5:03pm. I am outside on a bench by the bushes where I stash my dirty clothes until I take them to laundry nearby. I decided to spend my birthday outside so that I can remind myself that I am still homeless, although I have been able to go indoors and sleep on my friend's couch or floor for a couple of weeks. I will be heading to my tent to meditate and reflect on my journey so far. Seems like I am seeing some light at the end of the tunnel, but I am still conscious of my current homeless situation while working hard to end it permanently. I have been homeless off-on for a long time. But now, with my writings, doors are opening. I am grateful. I am not complaining. This meal is delicious, blessed be the sister who prepared it out of compassion and pure kindness. Leo

December 2020

-2:00pm. I made my appointment with the dentist at SOME dental clinic for the homeless. Time for dentures. Last year, I had about 10 teeth pulled. I was in the process of getting dentures when the Coronavirus pandemic shut everything down. So I am getting back with the process and hopefully, I can be able to properly chew again and eat some of the food I like but can't eat now. I am glad I can my book and buy my own food so that I won't rely on food from soup kitchens that may not be able to properly digest. I am grateful. While at the same time, I want to let you know that dental care although available for the homeless in Washington DC, is still a concern. Hopefully more homeless have access to dental care. And I am grateful for places like SOME dental clinic here in Washington DC. They doing a good job.

February 2021

-The air outside is so fresh and pure. I feel like in heaven walking outside in the snow. Tomorrow is another day. Hopefully, tomorrow will give birth to good news. Hopefully, I wake up to see tomorrow. We shouldn't take anything for granted in this life. Every second we are still here on this earth is something we should be grateful for. Leo

-Some angel is willing to rent me an apartment. Thank you to everyone who supported me and my book. I have saved as much as I could so I would no longer have to sleep outside or on somebody's couch or floor. I am grateful to you all. Although it is not finalized yet, I am in the process of renting an apartment from a landlord, who is willing to rent to a homeless man who only relies on selling his book as an income. I call this a miracle.

-Tomorrow I am picking up keys for my apartment. I just signed the lease and will pick the keys tomorrow. There are fixtures to be made on Monday. But I will be working on getting some furniture this weekend. Landlord asked for the first month and security deposit. I went ahead and paid first and last month's rents plus security deposit, therefore 3 months of rent. The transition will not be easy because I have been a chronic homeless, meaning for more than 10 years (Off and on though). The trauma I endured for so long, of homelessness will not dissipate overnight.

-5:00pm. Sleeping in my own bed, in my own place is so therapeutic. I feel like I am in a hospital recuperating. Wow, my whole body and mind are feeling the effect of real rest and relief and healing.

-11:45 am. I woke up a couple of hours ago in a place where I can call my own as long as I pay my rent every month. I have been a chronic homeless off and on for so long that I am ashamed to say. For the last 3 months, I slept on my friend's couch and floor. But for a little over 5 years, I lived in a tent that I set up in a wooded area, away from everybody. I had so many nightmares, some time back to back the same day, that I was scared to go back to sleep. Sometimes, I would dream that I was in a nice place, but woke up back in a tent.

-When I used to go out by old Ebbitt's grill, on 25th and G North West, Washington dc, right around the corner to the White House, my goal was to save enough to get me a nice place. Although, I could sell at least two books in an hour (I was selling my book for $10 a copy on the street), I was not able to save enough to even think about trying to find a place to rent. But because of covid 19, I was forced to activate my website and focus on selling my book online. When on my birthday, I decided to do a fundraiser to get rid of 100 books I had stored at my friend's place, so many of you responded by ordering a bit over a thousand in 2 days November 22 and especially, November 23). Today it is because of the generosity, kindness, and support of all of you, that I am in a warm place of my own this morning while it is snowing this morning. I want to thank every single of you who have supported me, either by ordering a copy or simply donated. And I apologize to the few of you who did not get their copies yet for reasons that I have already explained and trying to correct so that there won't be future occurrences. I want you to know, I am so grateful to you. Thank you one thousand times.

I want to end with this one.

-Here goes the sun rising. Which means that I woke up to see a new day. My first reaction is, I am blessed and grateful to have been allowed to be alive and see another day. My second reaction is, how to make it a

179

productive day? If you are still alive, you are blessed. Don't worry about the little issues you have to face today. Just try your best and be happy you still here. Enjoy your day. Leo Gnawa

.

Made in the USA
Middletown, DE
02 July 2021